ORIGAMI
ZOO

ORIGAMI ZOO

An Amazing Collection of Folded Paper Animals

Robert J. Lang and
Stephen Weiss

ST. MARTIN'S PRESS
New York

Design by Richard Oriolo
Cover photo by Marcel Cataldo
Cover design by Russell Gordon

Library of Congress Cataloging-in-Publication Data
Lang, Robert J.
    Origami zoo : an amazing collection of folded paper animals /
Robert J. Lang & Stephen Weiss
        p.   cm.
    ISBN 0-312-04015-6
    1. Origami.   2. Animals in art.   I. Weiss, Stephen.
II. Title.
TT870.L262   1990
736'.982—dc20   89-77959
                                                          CIP

First Edition

10 9 8 7 6 5 4 3

CONTENTS

ACKNOWLEDGMENTS

The authors would like to thank the following people for their generous assistance in the production of this book: Samuel Randlett for thoughtful advice and extensive editing of the manuscript; John Montroll and Peter Engel for fruitful discussions on origami design and diagramming; Arthur and Janice Weiss for supplying photographic equipment; Marcel Cataldo and Anthony Zebrowski for assistance with the photography; Arnold Tubis for translating Japanese publishing information; Diane Lang for editing, suggestions, and moral support; and our editor, Barbara Anderson, and her assistant, Marian Lizzi, for their skillful and sensitive handling of the manuscript.

INTRODUCTION

The Japanese word *origami* is a compound of *ori* (to fold) and *kami* (paper). Although origami has been a part of Japanese culture for more than a thousand years, it began in China, the birthplace of paper. (A tradition of paper folding in Spain, independent for many centuries, is presumed to derive from the Moorish occupation, and ultimately from the Orient.)

Many countries, including the United States, have a modest tradition of origami: The "fortune teller," paper airplanes, boats, and hats one learns to fold in childhood are typical examples. Until recently, however, the world repertoire of origami designs remained limited and static; the same few dozen models were passed down through the generations. This began to change some fifty years ago when a young man in Japan named Akira Yoshizawa started to create new models. (Although original works by Montero in Spain and Solorzano and Montoya in Argentina were being invented at about this time, they were not circulated widely outside their country of origin.) As Yoshizawa's books of origami were published, other people grasped the possibilities and began to design models of their own—and the ancient art of paper folding was reborn.

East and West alike participated in this renaissance, which transformed a traditional pastime into a vigorous new art form. Through a stream of books, magazine articles, and holiday displays, the public has become increasingly aware of origami; active societies such as The Friends of the Origami Center of America have been organized all over the world (see Sources, page 165). Folders have used many novel and ingenious techniques to produce thousands of different models. There are action models—birds that flap their wings, frogs that jump, figures that tumble and rock, "talking" masks, swimming dolphins, fiddling violinists, pinwheels, noisemakers, and gliding airplanes. There are functional models such as envelopes, boxes, vases, hats, bookmarks, purses, wallets, rings, cups, even slippers. There are purely ornamental folds, some of them constructed from many interlocking units ("modular origami"). There are models designed specifically to be folded from dollar bills. Animal models, with their semblance of life, remain the most popular, and the original works in this book, created within the last ten years, comprise an eclectic zoological garden gathered from land, water, air, and the realms of myth.

The noted architect Frank Lloyd Wright observed that "the human race built most nobly when limitations were greatest and, therefore, when most was required of imagination. . . . Limitations have always been the best friend of architecture." The same might be said about paper folding. A good part of the appeal of origami is the challenge of creating an elegant little sculpture (a dog, perhaps, or a camel) without violating the stringent principles of the craft, for origami, though it yields a tangible result, is a kind of game. The strictest rules of this game allow only the folding of a single square of paper. A slight relaxation of the rules allows the use of rectangles, triangles, and other convex polygons; more liberal yet is the use of peculiar shapes or multiple sheets of paper. Cutting, gluing, and decorating are considered poor form but even these may on occasion have their place, depending on the purpose and strength of the effect. In this book, each design is folded from a single sheet of paper, usually a square, without gluing or cutting.

The strict rules serve both to stimulate creativity and to impose on origami models a general style of great economy and power. Within the rules and within the general style there is, however, a surprising amount of room for individual differences, and each creative folder blends vision with method in a uniquely personal way.

People easily and naturally incline to assume that the origami books or models with which they are acquainted mark the limits of the art of paper folding. The truth is that all the paper-folding books ever published represent only a small fraction of the designs that have been created, and these in turn are only an intimation of what is yet possible.

GETTING STARTED

HOW TO USE THIS BOOK

FOLLOWING THE INSTRUCTIONS

Before folding the models in this book, first study the explanation of the symbols and procedures on pages 9–24. Refer back to this section whenever necessary. The models range in complexity from fairly simple to advanced and are presented in that order. The instructions are intended to help build skills and teach techniques in a sequential way.

Each drawing shows two things: the result of the previous step, and the action to be taken next. Before performing the operation immediately shown, look ahead to the next step, or next several steps, to see what the result will be.

On the first drawing of some models, crease lines divide the paper in half horizontally, vertically, or diagonally. These are always assumed to be valley folds and should be made before the first step begins.

Written instructions are provided for each step and should be used with the drawings. In this book, wherever the word *fold* is used by itself to describe an action, it means *valley-fold*. The terms *upper, lower, top, bottom, left, right, horizontal,* and *vertical* refer to the dimensions of the page itself: Thus "toward the top" means "toward the top of the page." The terms *front* and *near* refer to location or motion perpendicular to the page, that is, toward the folder; the terms *far, behind,* and *back* refer to location or motion away from the folder. The terms *in* and *inward* mean toward the middle of the model; the terms *out* and *outward* mean away from the middle.

FOLDING

Origami is a geometrical art, and for this reason there is little tolerance for error in the folding process. Small inaccuracies at the beginning turn into large ones as the sequence progresses. Folding on a hard, flat surface is the best way to get sharp creases and precise results. Creases may be given an extra sharpness if necessary by running a thumbnail over the folded edge. Where the instructions indicate that edges (or points) are to be brought together, align the points or edges carefully and—holding them firmly in place—flatten and crease the paper. Where two points are to be connected by a crease, fold the paper over to make small pinch marks through the points (thus determining the position of the line that is to be formed), and then crease through the pinch marks. Soft creases have their place in origami, too—the appeal of many models can be enhanced by subtle shaping, rounding, and adjustment of the finished form.

PAPER

Many different types of paper can be used for origami. The choice depends on the type and size of the model to be folded, the finished appearance desired, and the available type of paper. Basically, any paper that can hold a crease and not tear or crack when folded back and forth is suitable. Some models are designed to use paper with a different color on each side to achieve a color contrast in the finished model. In this book the drawings for such designs are toned accordingly. Commercial origami paper comes in packages of precut sheets, 3 to 10 inches square, usually white on one side and colored on the other side. Some types have multicolored patterns on one side, or a different color on each side. For larger sheets of two-tone paper, various gift-wrapping papers can be cut to the desired size. An accurate paper cutter, the larger the better, or a razor blade and carpenter's square, is very useful for this. (Paper cutters are sold by office supply stores, and—as print trimmers—by photographic supply houses.) Just as inaccurate folding will produce an unsatisfactory result, so too will inaccurately cut paper. A square must be exactly square; a rectangle or triangle must have the exact proportion required.

Some origami models look best when folded from paper that can be molded and can hold its shape. Paper-backed foil, such as gift wrap, works very well for this and is easy to use, although crease marks, once made, are indelible. Look for high-quality paper-backed foils; the color shouldn't fade from light or rub off along creases, the foil shouldn't crack when folded back and forth, and there should be no objectionable odor from glue or glaze. Another possibility is florist's foil, which is green on one side and silver, gold, or another color on the reverse side. It contains no paper: the foil is bonded to a thin plastic film, making it malleable, waterproof, and forgiving of extraneous creases. (The Alligator on the cover and on page 77 is folded from florist's foil.)

It is also possible to make your own foil-backed paper, by bonding tissue to both sides of ordinary household aluminum foil using spray adhesive (available in office and photographic supply stores). The resulting paper is very workable, and the combination of the translucent tissue and reflective foil gives a slightly mottled texture with the appearance of depth. Such a paper is suited for insect constructions and small, complex folds that require much shaping.

There is a technique in origami called *wet folding* that is especially suitable for models that involve a lot of shaping (many of the models in the photographs were wet-folded). Wet folding requires heavy artist's or drafting paper that contains sizing; the sheet is dampened with a wet cloth or a fine spray before and during folding in order to allow sculpted shaping that becomes rigid when the paper dries. The effect is similar to that obtained with foil except that the model is much sturdier and, for animals, appears more natural. To achieve a natural effect with paper-backed foil, the paper side can be colored (or left white) before folding and then used as the outside of the model—(see, for example, the photographs of the Woolly Mammoth, on the cover and on page 93, and the Reindeer, page 137).

These are certainly not the only possibilities. Papers found in office, artist's, craft, and packaging supply stores provide a variety of different colors, weights, and textures. For a source of a wide selection of precut origami paper, see The Friends of the Origami Center of America, page 165.

DESIGNING

There are several ways to go about designing an origami model. The basic methods are improvisation, alteration of an existing model, and systematic design.

Much of the recorded origami literature was developed through improvisation. The improviser plays with a piece of paper until it begins to resemble something. Only rarely will such a suggestive resemblance constitute a finished model—the paper must be engineered toward the goal suggested by the paper itself, and thus at a certain point free exploration merges with conscious design. There are several traditional bases—regular geometric folded shapes—that lend themselves to improvisatory manipulation, but the four "classic" bases (Kite, Fish, Bird, and Frog) have been so thoroughly explored that it is difficult to develop a substantially new design from them. This book, however, will help with that problem, because it contains many new bases that have yet to be systematically explored.

The second method is to take a model that someone else has invented and change it. The ethics of folding dictate that you must change it substantially to call it your own model. Turning a reindeer into a moose, for example, does not make it yours. If, however, you turn a deer into an eagle, that is sufficiently different to call it your own creation. This metamorphosis, by the way, is not as hard as it may sound. Mammals and birds have four limbs; two deer legs could be changed into the eagle's wings, and the body altered, through shaping.

This shaping, which turns a flap into a leg, wing, or head or otherwise refines the form, can be accomplished with the basic folds shown in Procedures, pages 16–24. Mountain and valley folds are the mainstay of shaping folds; they can change the direction of a flap, narrow a point, blunt a sharp point, and add edges and lines to a shape. Reverse folds can accomplish the same things as mountain and valley folds, but more symmetrically and in some cases more permanently. A flap that has been turned at a right angle with a reverse fold is less likely to come unfolded than one that has been simply mountain- or valley-folded. Petal folds both narrow and lengthen points; a swivel fold (which is really just half of a petal fold) accomplishes the same thing. Rabbit ear folds convert wide flaps into narrow points. Crimps and pleats shorten points, change their directions, and add lines and edges that can define important features that are not actually appendages (especially heads and faces). Sinks can hide unwanted points or edges inside the model.

The third method of design is to use a systematic approach to create a model "from the ground up." Essentially, it consists of developing a special-purpose base for each subject. A *base* is a regular geometric shape that has a structure similar to that of the subject, although it may actually appear to bear very little resemblance to the subject. The design of a base must take into account the entire sheet of paper. All parts of a base are linked together and cannot be altered without affecting the rest of the paper. On the other hand, the shaping folds, those folds that transform the appearance of the base into the final model, usually affect only a small part of the paper. Converting a base into an animal using shaping folds requires tactical thinking. Developing the base to begin with requires strategy.

In selecting or designing a base, consider the number and size of points needed for appendages. You may be able to use tactical folds to develop some of the smaller points, such as ears or a tail, or even some of the larger ones (by crimping and pleating, for example). The general shape of the subject and the way in which a base conforms to it must also be considered, although some simple manipulations can alter the shape of a base dramatically.

There are groups of symmetries and techniques that allow the designer to get any desired assembly of appendages. One of these groups is called box pleating. It is typified by rows of parallel creases that divide the paper (or a portion of the paper) into a grid of squares, and occasional creases at 45 degrees to those. Box pleating may be used for models made from squares, but the technique is especially suited to rectangles. To design a new model with box pleating, imagine an infinitely long rectangle. Divide it along the short side into eighths, twelfths, or sixteenths; each division is defined as one unit. Beginning at one end of the rectangle, lay out the parts of the subject along the length of the rectangle, allocating appropriate amounts of paper for each appendage (for example, a pair of opposing three-unit-long points requires six units of paper). When you've allocated paper for all the parts, cut off the excess, and you'll have the starting rectangle. Crease all the horizontal and vertical unit divisions; crease the diagonals; then, starting from one end, collapse the paper by pleating both horizontally and vertically at the same time to form a base.

Box pleating has been used to produce some of the most fantastic structures yet seen in origami: a working jack-in-the-box, an action cuckoo clock, a steam locomotive, cars, trains, planes, a man with a guitar, and a matador fighting a bull, to name a few. While the rectilinear lines of a box-pleated model are well suited for man-made objects—and in fact, most box-pleated models are inanimate—there are many animals (including human figures) that have been designed using this technique. Box pleating is used in the Butterfly and Frog; and to make the body, hind legs, and tail of the Fox; the body and legs of the Alligator; and the antlers of the Reindeer.

Another group of symmetries has its roots in the classic bases, starting with the Kite Base. It is typified by creases at 22.5 degrees to each other, and repetition of the same basic shapes at different sizes, in powers of $\sqrt{2}$ and $1 + \sqrt{2}$. This set of techniques is generally more versatile for animal models, especially those with many appendages. It appears in the Praying Mantis, Crab, Horsefly, Black Widow, Mouse, Collie, Camel, Golden Eagle, Rabbit, Duck, Dolphin, Roadrunner, and the fronts of the Dog in a Doghouse and Woolly Mammoth.

Even systematic design using these techniques is not perfect, however. It is common to set the design constraints and construct a base with the required appendages, only to find it thick or awkward. This can sometimes be avoided by designing with what might be called idiosyncratic systemization—that is, folding that does not follow any particular set of geometric symmetries; the geometry, such as there is, is determined by the desired shape instead of the shape being determined by the geometry. Examples of this are the Giraffe, Irish Setter, Skunk, Penguin, and, to some degree, the Rabbit. Idiosyncratic systemization, although not always elegant in the process itself, is often very efficient—in fact, it can be far more efficient than a purely geometric rendering of a similar base.

One way to use this method is to decide, disregarding geometry, where the points should be on the edges of the paper to achieve the greatest efficiency for the number and length of appendages required, and then collapse the paper into a base so that all the points are narrowed and defined, hiding the excess paper in pleats. A disadvantage to this approach is that if there are many such pleats of random sizes, the surface of the model can look messy and irregular. It is possible, however, to align the edges of some pleats and hide the rest (for example, by forming them on the inside of the model—see the Giraffe, page 120) and to achieve a base with lines as simple and clean as any derived from a geometric approach.

Most models, however, use not one, but rather a mixture of different design techniques. The Reindeer, Fox, and Alligator, for example, mix box pleating with kite-type folds; the Rabbit mixes kite-type folds with idiosyncratic systemization.

Much of a model's design is specific to that model, but there are usually parts that are adaptable to other circumstances. By studying the designs of others, you can learn new techniques and ideas to apply to your own creations. The origami presented here will help you in this regard, not just because it includes the ideas of two people, but because the models incorporate techniques from still more people. The Camel and Collie, for example, use techniques similar to those of John Montroll in *Origami for the Enthusiast* (New York: Dover, 1979), in *Animal Origami for the Enthusiast* (New York: Dover, 1985), and in *Origami Sculptures* (Bethesda, Md.: Antroll, 1989). The Butterfly shares its overall structure (although not its symmetry) with one by Peter Engel in *Folding the Universe* (New York: Random House, 1989, pages 292–311). Box-pleating techniques such as those in the Frog were extensively explored by Neal Elias in pioneering work in the 1960s and 1970s. As others have influenced our work, so they may influence yours.

When you fold using others' techniques, chances are that eventually you will duplicate someone else's work. Don't worry about it. What may be common ground at one point can diverge at the next. An example of this is the Frog, the base of which is extremely suggestive of its subject. Exactly the same base was developed independently in Japan by Kōshō Uchiyama and is used for a frog published in his book *Junsui Origami* (*Pure Origami*; Tokyo: Kokuda Sha, 1979, pages 132–136). Even though they share the same base, these two frogs are finished in much different ways (see Figure 1). If the base were more ambiguous, completely different animals might have been developed. This case

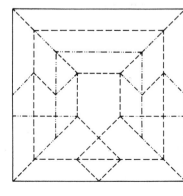

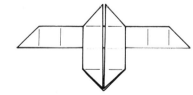

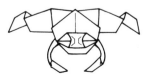

Figure 1: The crease pattern, base, and folded examples of (right) Uchiyama's Frog and (bottom) Weiss's frog.

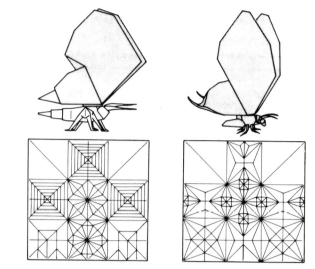

Figure 2: (left) Lang's Butterfly and its crease pattern; (right) Engel's butterfly and its crease pattern.

shows how detail or tactical folding can create different styles of a subject from the same base. In the case of the two butterflies (see Figure 2), the final appearances are fairly similar; the style difference is reflected more in the strategy of folding. Engel's Butterfly is based strongly on kite-type folding; the one in this book is mostly box-pleated. Of course, models of the same subject can vary in both technical style and visual aspect.

One useful stylistic choice is to create a design illusion that simplifies the subject. This method can be both effective and efficient. For example, the Squirrel (see page 62) really has only one ear; a cupping gives the impression of depth. To redesign the Squirrel to get two separate points for the ears would produce a different model altogether because, in this case, two proper ears cannot be obtained by tactical folding. Although many of the models in this book are highly detailed, as illustrated by the legs and antennae of the Butterfly (see page 143), it is not always necessary, or even desirable, to achieve "teeth and claws" realism. Simple models have the virtue of clean, uncluttered lines. Sacrificing realism for elegance can free the design to be more interpretive or expressive. The Dolphin (see page 27), for example, has only a single point for a tail, rather than a pair of horizontal flukes (as in the real animal); the model, however, is a simple caricature of the subject featuring an action mechanism and makes no attempt at anatomical verisimilitude. Representing a leg by a crimp can create an artistic impression with minimal folding; the Gorilla (see page 36), too, is more abstract. The goal is a suggestion of a gorilla, not a photograph.

Finally, discovering folding possibilities and designing new models are not dependent on completing every model in this book. In fact, several creative masters developed substantial bodies of work in isolation, having known only a few traditional folds. As you progress through these models, feel free at any time to explore your own creative urges, be they merely to manipulate interesting shapes or to develop a subject systematically. If you have trouble achieving a particular result, don't give up immediately. Try a different maneuver or approach. Check to see if perhaps another subject is lurking in the folds. Put the work aside for a while and pick it up again later. Sometimes a model can be designed in minutes, or it may take weeks or even years. Whenever you complete it, it will be your own unique contribution to this fascinating art.

SYMBOLS

Over the past thirty years, a code of symbols has been developed to communicate origami. The original symbols were developed by the Japanese master Akira Yoshizawa in the 1950s and have been refined further as new and unforeseen requirements arose. To an experienced folder, the origami symbols form a rich and powerful language. Fortunately for the novice, most of them are rather suggestive of their meaning. In this section we show twenty-two basic symbols that are used throughout this book. It is strongly recommended that you take a few minutes to study these symbols and the procedures in the next section, before attempting the models.

VALLEY FOLD

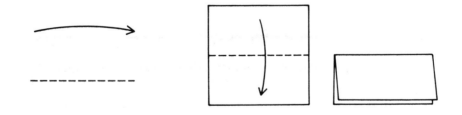

When a flap or layer of paper is folded so that the crease forms a trough, that is called a valley fold. A valley fold is indicated by a dashed line, and an arrow with a symmetric split head shows the motion of the paper. In this example, the top of the paper is folded down to meet the bottom, making a valley fold.

MOUNTAIN FOLD

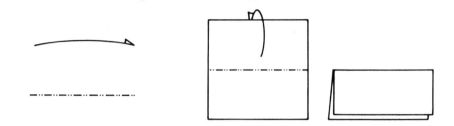

When a flap or layer of paper is folded away from you so that the crease forms a peak, that is called a mountain fold. A mountain fold is indicated by a chain line (two dots alternating with a dash) and an arrow with a one-sided hollow head showing the motion of the paper. In general, if the arrow has a split head, the paper starts out moving toward you; if the head is hollow, the paper moves away from you.

FOLD AND UNFOLD

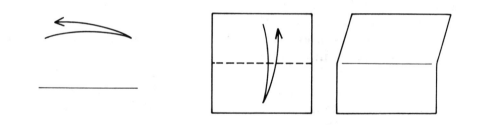

When an arrow doubles back on itself, that is the sign to fold the paper as indicated and then unfold it. The paper would thus end up in the configuration in which it started, except it would have a crease where it had been folded. Creases are indicated by thinner lines than edges, as shown; where a crease meets an edge, there will be a small gap, to emphasize its presence and further differentiate it from an edge.

PUSH HERE

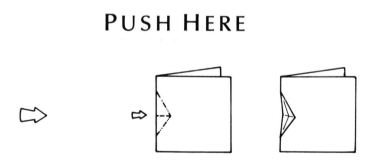

A small, hollow arrow with a flat tail indicates "push here." Usually, that means that rather than being folded toward or away from you, the paper is pushed in symmetrically, or even inverted. For more examples of this, see the Inside Reverse Fold, page 17, the Petal Folds, page 22, and the Sinks, pages 23–24.

EDGE CONFIGURATIONS

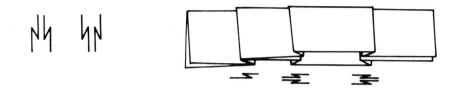

When a flap with several layers is folded in a short zigzag, there is actually more than one way that the layers can be arranged: the entire flap can be folded back and forth (as on the left), or it can be folded inside itself and back out (as on the right). To distinguish these cases, zigzag lines are drawn next to the model to symbolize an edge-on view (compare the edges of the bottom of the figure to the zigzag line or lines below it).

WATCH THIS SPOT

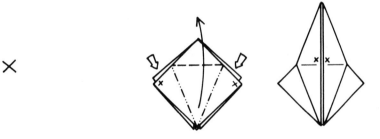

If an unusual step is occurring (the illustration is a petal fold, page 22), seeing where the spot marked with an X goes can clarify the movement of the paper.

ROTATE

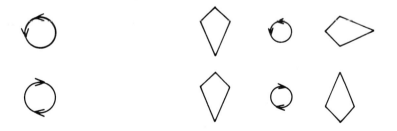

Rotation of the model is shown by a circle with two arrowheads on it. The arrows show the direction of rotation (counterclockwise or clockwise); the spacing of the two arrowheads indicates the degree of rotation, such as a quarter or a half turn.

EQUAL DISTANCES

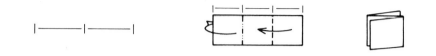

If the folds are to be made so that two or more distances are equal, the distances are marked with this symbol.

EQUAL ANGLES

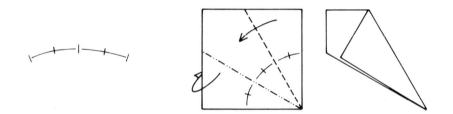

If two or more angles are meant to be equal, they are marked off by similar arcs.

FOLD OVER AND OVER

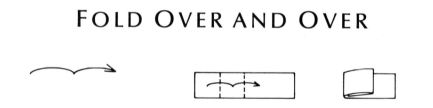

An arrow that "touches down" more than once indicates to valley-fold once, and then valley-fold again (and again, if necessary, for as many times as the arrow touches down).

OPEN SINK

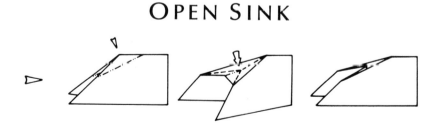

This is a very specific way of inverting a point so that it flattens out completely when it is halfway done (see Procedures, page 23). An open sink is indicated by a stemless hollow arrowhead.

CLOSED SINK

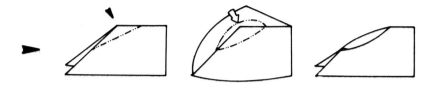

In this less common fold, the point is inverted *without* coming unfolded partway through. When it is complete, the edges will be locked together (see Procedures, page 24). A closed sink is indicated by a stemless solid arrowhead.

TURN THE PAPER OVER

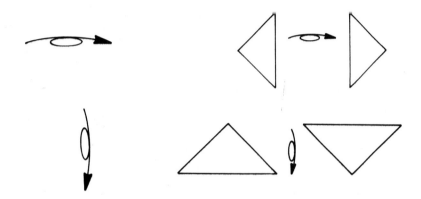

An arrow that makes a loop means to turn over the entire model. If the arrow runs horizontally, the paper should be turned over from side to side. If it runs vertically, the paper should be turned over from top to bottom.

PULL PAPER OUT FROM HERE

A hollow arrow with a cleft tail indicates to pull out some paper from an interior pocket or in some way to unfold some paper. The arrow will emerge from the place where the paper is to be pulled out.

CUT-AWAY VIEW

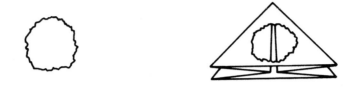

A jagged line is used to give a view of hidden layers of paper, drawn as if the near layers of paper were torn away to expose the inner layers.

X-RAY LINE

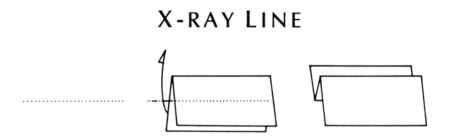

A dotted line is used to indicate a fold or an edge that is hidden, and in this respect is similar to the cut-away view. Typically, an X-ray line will be used to indicate the continuation of a fold behind a flap, while the cut-away view is used to show more complicated structures. This example also shows that the mountain-fold line may be extended past the edge of the paper if there's not enough of it showing otherwise. Occasionally an X-ray line is used to show the projected position that an edge will assume in the next step.

NEXT VIEW LARGER

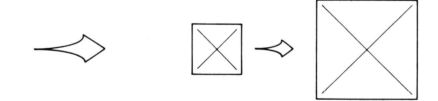

A hollow expanding arrow indicates that the next drawing represents an enlarged view.

Next View from this Vantage Point

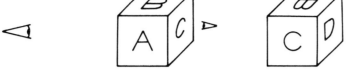

In three-dimensional models, a view from the side of a model is indicated by this stylized eye; the next illustration is drawn from the point of view of an observer looking at the model from the location and in the direction of the symbol.

Hold Here and Pull

A small circle with an arrow attached to it means to hold the paper at the circle (usually between thumb and forefinger) and to pull in the direction of the arrow. These may come in pairs, indicating where to hold the paper with each hand.

PROCEDURES

WATERBOMB BASE

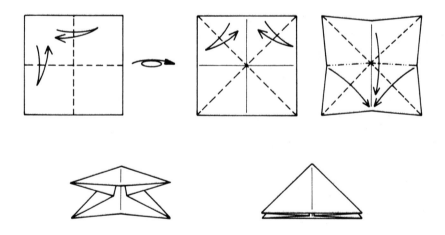

The Waterbomb Base is a basic shape used in many traditional folds. To make it, first crease the paper in half vertically and horizontally; then turn the paper over. Now crease it in half along both diagonals. Bring the middle of all four sides together and flatten the paper out with two flaps going in each direction.

PRELIMINARY FOLD

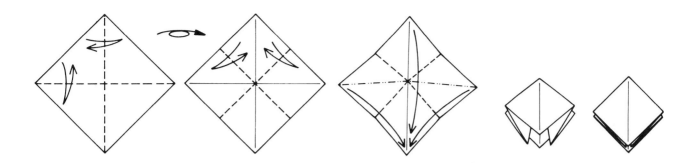

The Preliminary Fold is another basic shape (which, because it is a stage in the folding of the Bird Base and the Frog Base, is called Preliminary Fold rather than Preliminary Base). It can be made by turning a Waterbomb Base inside out, or it can be made directly this way. Crease the diagonals of the square first; then turn the paper over and crease it in half the other way. Bring all four corners together and flatten out the paper with two flaps falling to the right and two to the left.

INSIDE REVERSE FOLD

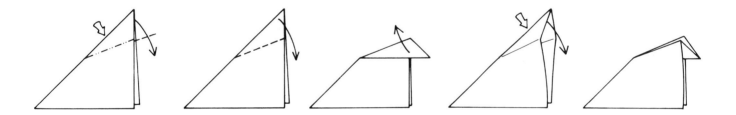

The inside reverse fold is a way of changing the direction of a flap that is more permanent than simply folding it over would be. An inside reverse fold is indicated by a mountain-fold line on the near layer of paper and a valley-fold line on the far layer if it is visible (first diagram). There is also a push arrow pointing to the spine of the fold. Inside reverse folds are usually referred to simply as reverse folds in this book.

To make an inside reverse fold, first fold the flap along the indicated fold line and unfold; this is to weaken the paper to make the reverse fold easier. To make the actual fold, spread the near and far layers of paper and push the spine of the moving flap down between them. The flap turns inside out in the process (hence the name *reverse fold*). Flatten the paper. As you become more experienced with origami, you will develop the ability to make reverse folds without precreasing, but if you are a beginner, it will always be easier if you precrease first.

OUTSIDE REVERSE FOLD

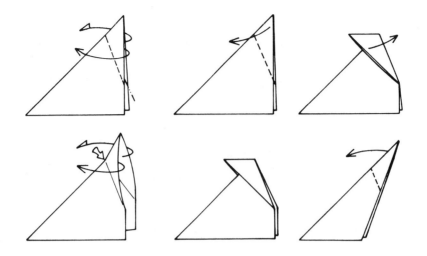

The outside reverse fold, which is closely related to the inside reverse fold, is also a way of changing the direction of a flap. While the inside reverse fold turns a flap toward its open edges, the outside reverse fold turns it in the opposite direction. An outside reverse fold is indicated by a valley fold on the near layer of paper (and a mountain fold on the far layer, if it is visible) and arrows showing the direction of motion of the paper (first diagram).

To make an outside reverse fold, first fold and unfold the flap along the intended crease line to weaken the paper. Then, spread the layers of the moving flap and wrap them around the rest of the model. Flatten the paper. As with the inside reverse fold, until you become more experienced, you should always precrease the fold. On narrow points where it is difficult to show both layers of an outside reverse fold, it will frequently be shown with only one arrow, as in the last diagram above.

INCORPORATING A REVERSE FOLD

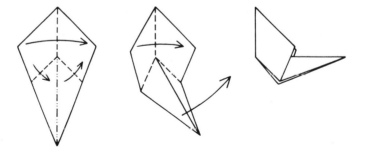

Sometimes in the book, a step will require you to "incorporate a reverse fold" while folding layers together. This is what is meant.

CRIMP

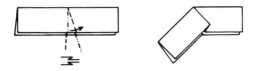

A crimp is used to change the direction of a flap or point, and to form features such as beaks, muzzles, ears, haunches, and feet. There are several types of crimps.

In the type of crimp shown above, the paper is swiveled from a spot on the folded edge and overlaps at the open edges. In this book, it is shown with an edge configuration symbol (see Symbols, page 11) next to the open edges.

In the type of crimp shown above, the paper overlaps only at the folded edge.

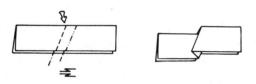

In this third case, above, the paper overlaps at both the folded edge and the open edges. The second and third pairs of crimps above are actually formed by making two sequential reverse folds, as below.

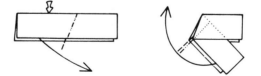

RABBIT EAR FOLD

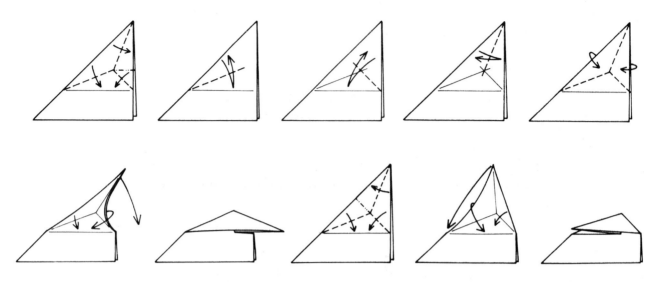

The rabbit ear is a way of narrowing a flap and changing its direction. It is indicated by three valley folds that meet at a point and a fourth mountain fold emanating from that point (first diagram, top row; and third diagram, bottom row). Nearly always, the flap is a triangle and the three valley folds bisect the angles of the triangle. The way to start, therefore, is to crease individually each of the angle bisectors. Then bring two sides of the flap together and pinch it in half. Swing the flap down to the side and flatten the paper.

As the diagrams show, a rabbit ear that uses the same valley folds can go in two different directions. In a model's instructions, arrows (and the location of the mountain fold) will show which way it goes.

The following diagrams show several of the different types of rabbit ears used in the book. (See also Double Rabbit Ear, page 23.)

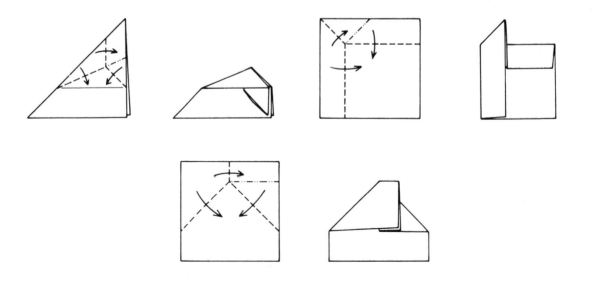

SQUASH FOLD

The squash fold is a way of converting one folded edge into two. It is indicated by valley and mountain fold lines and a push arrow pointing to the edge to be squashed (first diagram). To make a squash fold, spread the open layers of the edge to be squashed and flatten them so that the edge ends up on top of the fold line at the base of the flap, as point X does in the example.

SWIVEL FOLD

This is a simple swivel. The swivel action is inherent in many pleats, crimps, and squash folds.

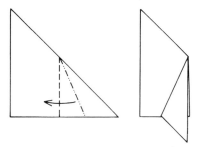

When a squash fold is made while swiveling an adjacent layer, a special kind of swivel fold results. This is shown below.

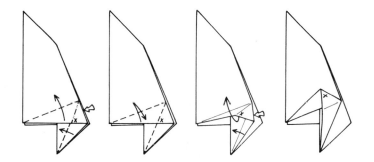

The swivel fold is a way of narrowing a flap without changing its direction. It is indicated by two valley folds that meet at a point with a mountain fold between them (first diagram). As with most of the other folds, it is most easily executed if you precrease the layers of paper. The two valley folds are then put in at the same time, and the mountain fold is formed when you flatten the paper, forming a collar. The region marked X in the example swivels upward —hence the name.

PETAL-FOLDING A POINT

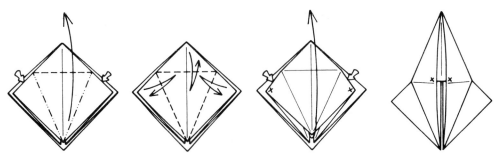

The petal fold is a means of simultaneously narrowing and lengthening a point. It is indicated by two mountain folds and a valley fold that form a triangle, with a push arrow on each side of the petal fold (first diagram). The mountain folds are nearly always angle bisectors, and when you precrease (as shown in the second diagram), you should crease the mountain folds first. Then, crease a valley fold that connects the mountain folds where they meet the outer edges. Next, lift up the point along the valley fold just made, and simultaneously push in the edges on the sides as shown. Watch the two points marked X; they end up meeting in the middle when the petal fold is completed.

PETAL-FOLDING AN EDGE

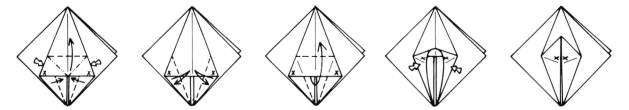

It is also possible to make a point out of an edge with a petal fold. This is indicated in the first diagram. To make this kind of petal fold, first crease the angle bisectors at the bottom (second diagram). Then fold the edge up along a valley fold that connects the top of the first two valley folds. Push in the sides and flatten the paper; two new valley folds that are formed will converge at a single point on the edge. Watch the points marked X; as the petal fold is made, they move in from the sides and finally meet in the center of the model.

INSIDE PETAL FOLD

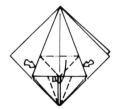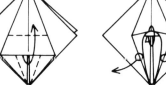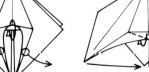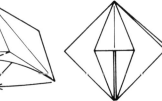

An inside petal fold is a modification of a conventional edge petal fold. It is indicated as in the first diagram. Precrease as for the conventional petal fold, and lift up the edge and bring the sides in as before (second diagram). Then, grasp the sides of the petal fold and pull them apart to each side; the edge moves back down. Push the middle of the edge up inside the model, bring the sides back together, and close the model again.

DOUBLE RABBIT EAR

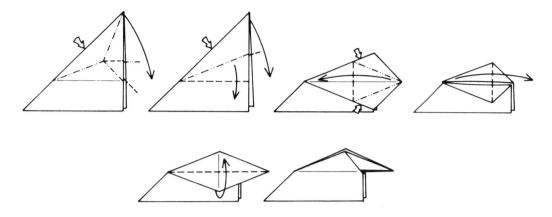

The double rabbit ear is a way of narrowing a point and changing its direction that is more secure than a conventional rabbit ear. (It bears the same relationship to a rabbit ear that a reverse fold does to a valley fold). It is indicated like a rabbit ear fold, except that the valley folds are replaced by mountain folds (and the short mountain fold becomes a valley fold), and a push arrow shows the direction of motion (first diagram). It may actually be performed in a single step, but it is easily done in two steps, as shown here. First, squash-fold the point in the indicated direction. Then, petal-fold the point to the left (in this example), and fold it back to the right without undoing the petal fold. Then fold the sides of the squashed area back together. The result is the same as if you had made two back-to-back rabbit ear folds.

OPEN SINK

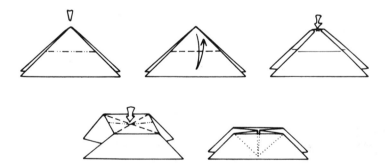

An open sink is a method of blunting a point that has no open edges and therefore cannot be reverse-folded. It is indicated by a hollow arrowhead directed at the point to be sunk and a mountain fold line that shows where the fold should be made (first diagram). To make an open sink, first crease the point firmly along the fold line. (It helps to crease it in both directions several times to further weaken the paper.) Then, gently pull apart the edges emanating from the point and push down on the very tip of the point, which should begin to flatten out. Continue flattening the tip, until the flattened region expands to the creases you made at the beginning; then push the middle of the point down and close the paper. When successfully completed, all of the edges will be visible at the top of the sink.

CLOSED SINK

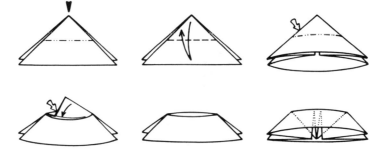

A closed sink is also a method of blunting a point; in addition it locks the edges of the point together. A closed sink is indicated by a filled arrowhead directed at the point to be sunk and a mountain fold line that shows where the fold should be made (first diagram). To make a closed sink, crease the point along the fold line the same as for an open sink. However, this time, instead of letting the top of the point open out flat, you must hold all of its layers together except for one layer that is spread apart from the rest, so that the point forms a conical shape. Then, beginning from one side, push down on an edge so that it starts to invert; the hard part is getting it started. Once the point starts to invert, push it all the way through until it is completely inverted. None of the interior edges are visible at the top of the completed closed sink. The last diagram shows the distribution of layers inside the model.

CLOSED WRAP

The closed wrap is closely related to the closed sink. The following three diagrams show how to fold a shape on which to practice.

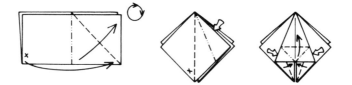

A closed wrap is indicated by an arrow that comes from behind a flap to the front of the flap; this denotes that the paper at the back of the flap should be brought to the front (first diagram). What distinguishes a closed wrap from other maneuvers in which paper is pulled out is that the paper behind the flap is continuous—there is no loose edge to grasp. To perform a closed wrap, push down on the flap with one hand and pull the layer of paper out from behind it; the corner of the flap turns inside out and forms a pocket. Then, wrap the pocket around the front of the flap and flatten the paper.

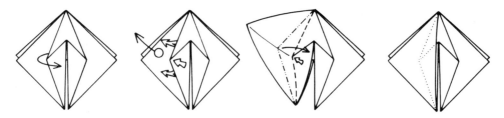

ORIGAMI
ZOO

DOLPHIN

Use a square the same color on both sides. If the paper is colored on one side only, begin with the white side up for a colored model. Crease the paper in half vertically.

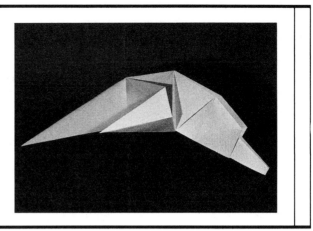

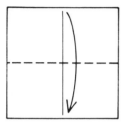

1. Fold the top edge down to the bottom edge.

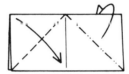

2. Fold the top left corner down to the middle of the bottom edge. Mountain-fold the top right corner to the middle of the bottom edge.

3. Spread the two long bottom edges apart, one toward you, the other away from you; simultaneously, push the sides toward each other and flatten the model.

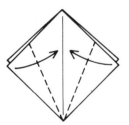

4. This is an enlarged side view of the result of step 3. This shape is called the *Preliminary Fold* (see Procedures, page 17). Fold the left and right corners of the near flaps so that their lower edges meet along the center line.

5. Fold the top point down over the edges of the flaps just folded and unfold. Unfold the two flaps in the middle, so that the paper returns to the configuration of step 4.

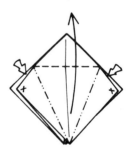

6. Lift up a single layer of paper on the horizontal crease remaining from the valley fold made in step 5; simultaneously, push in the edges of the near layers where shown. The raw edges of the left and right corners move in to the center line. Watch the points marked X. This is a *petal fold* (see Procedures, page 22).

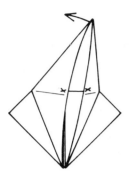

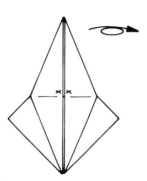

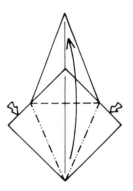

7. This shows the petal fold in progress. Flatten the paper.

8. Turn the paper over from side to side.

9. Petal-fold this side (it will be easier if you repeat the precreases in steps 4 and 5 first).

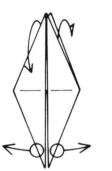

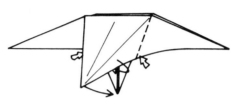

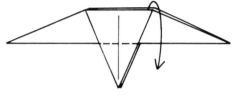

10. This shape is called the Bird Base. Bring the near top point slightly toward you and move the far top point slightly away; then grasp the tips of the two bottom points and pull them away from each other as far as they will go. The near and far top points will end up pointing downward and the middle of the paper will snap downward between them.

11. Push in the paper where the valley fold is shown on the right (and similarly on the left) and flatten the paper; repeat behind.

12. This is called the Stretched Bird Base. Fold one layer downward.

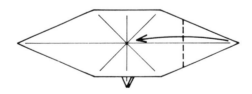

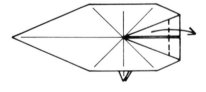

13. Fold the right point to the intersection of creases in the middle of the model.

14. Fold about ⅘ of the point back to the right.

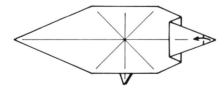

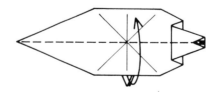

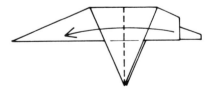

15. Fold the tip of the point back to the left.

16. Fold a single layer upward on the horizontal center line crease.

17. Fold the model in half from right to left on an existing vertical crease.

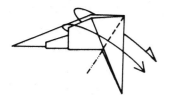

18. Fold the near flap down and to the right; the crease runs from the upper right corner to the vertex of the angle at center bottom. Mountain-fold the longer (far) flap behind along the same line.

19. Lift only one flap out from inside the model. (The central crease of this flap will invert itself: the valley fold will turn into a mountain fold.)

20. Fold one flap back to the left.

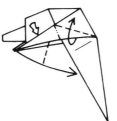

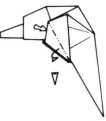

21. Fold another flap up to the left along the same line.

22. The head of the Dolphin is at the left; the tail extends down to the right; the fins are the flaps just under the head. *Squash-fold* the near fin down and to the right, lifting the right portion of its lower edge up toward the top of the model (see Procedures, page 20). The tip of the fin should touch the bottom edge of the model. Repeat behind.

23. Pinch the near fin in half and simultaneously pull it toward you, so that its cross section is a right angle and it stands straight out from the body.

24. The model looks like this from the bottom.

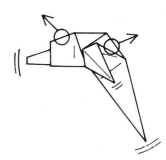

25. The finished Dolphin. Hold the head and the back where shown (be sure to hold all of the layers covered by the "hold here" circles) and pull the head and back in opposite directions. The Dolphin will "swim" with the motion of its fins and body.

PENGUIN

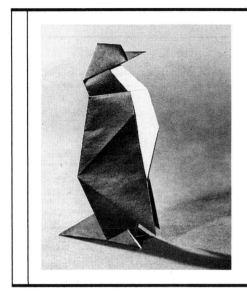

Use a square, black on one side and white on the other. Begin with the white side up. Crease the diagonals, making the vertical crease a mountain and the horizontal crease a valley.

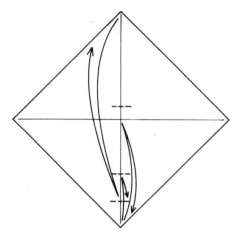

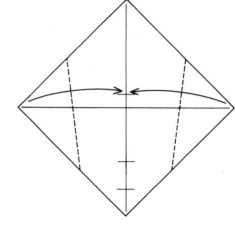

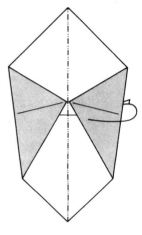

1. First fold the bottom corner up to touch the middle of the paper; pinch at the center of the crease and unfold. Second, fold the bottom corner up to touch that crease; pinch at the center and unfold. Third, fold the top corner down to touch that crease; pinch, and unfold.

2. Fold each of the side corners in to touch the point at which the last crease made crosses the vertical center crease.

3. Mountain-fold the right half of the paper.

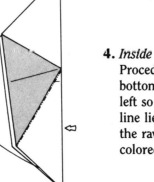

4. *Inside reverse-fold* (see Procedures, page 17) the bottom corner up to the left so that the crease line lies exactly beneath the raw edge of the colored flap.

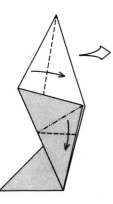

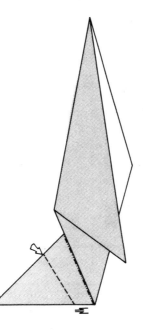

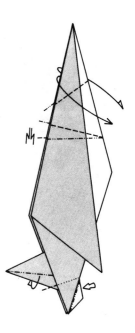

5. Swivel the corner down as you fold the left edge over to the right; the mountain fold is on an existing crease. Repeat behind.

6. Enlarged view. Reverse-fold the bottom left flap in and out.

7. *Outside-reverse-fold* (see Procedures, page 18) the top of the model to form a head. *Crimp* (see Procedures, page 19) the neck backward. Mountain-fold the bottom of the tail up inside as you flatten the edge at the right with a *swivel fold* (see Procedures, page 21). Repeat the last fold behind.

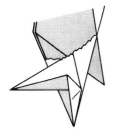

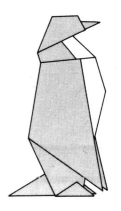

8. Cut-away view, showing the completed swivel fold.

9. Crimp the front of the head to form a beak. Fold over the corners inside the back to the near and far sides, respectively, to lock the neck in place. Crimp the foot upward; repeat behind.

10. The finished Penguin.

SWAN

Use a square, white on both sides. Crease the horizontal diagonal.

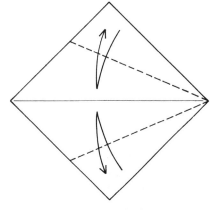

1. Fold the upper and lower right edges to the center line to form a Kite Base; unfold.

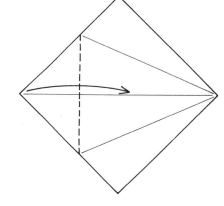

2. Fold the left corner of the square over to the right, forming a vertical crease that connects the intersections of the two creases made in step 1 with the edges of the square.

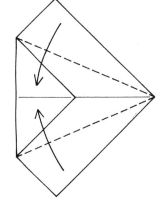

3. Refold the upper and lower right sides on the creases made in step 1.

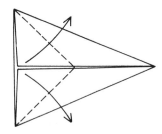

4. Fold the two loose corners at the left up and down, respectively, so that the creases formed lie exactly on the raw edges of the original left corner of the square.

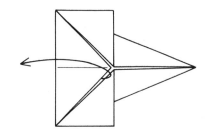

5. Unfold the corner.

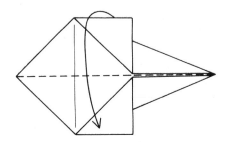

6. Fold the model in half lengthwise, top to bottom.

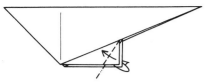 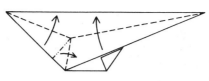

7. Fold the right edge of the protruding lower flap to the folded edges above it; repeat behind.

8. Fold a *rabbit ear* from the near side, bringing the lower edges of the large triangle to the upper edge (see Procedures, page 20); repeat behind.

9. Raise the neck by making an outside reverse fold that starts where the doubled layers inside (shown with X-ray lines) meet the top edge of the neck. Adjust the neck angle to match step 10.

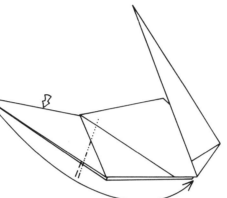

10. Enlarged view. Reverse-fold the point at the left (the tail) so that the tip just touches the corners formed by the bottom of the body and the base of the neck.

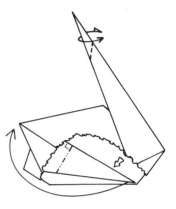

11. Reverse-fold the tail (shown here in cut-away view) back to the left so that it extends slightly beyond the rest of the model. Outside-reverse-fold the top of the neck to form a head.

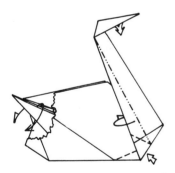

12. Cut-away view of the tail. Pull down the single layer on each side of the tail; opening the tail area slightly makes this easier. Narrow the neck by mountain-folding the back edge inside, swiveling up the bottom corner at the same time; repeat behind. Pull down the single layer on each side of the head from the inside.

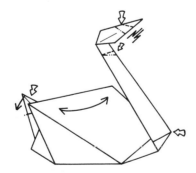

13. Form a beak with two reverse folds. Make a crimp on the neck below the head. Spread the tail somewhat by pressing down on the tip. Push in the front slightly to make the breast three-dimensional. Curve the wings slightly as shown.

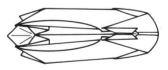
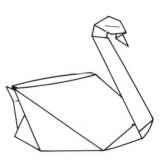

14. Two views of finished Swan.

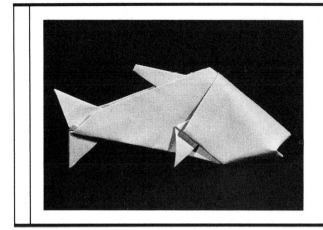

FISH

Use a square the same color on both sides. If the square is colored on one side only, begin with the white side up for a colored model. Crease the diagonals.

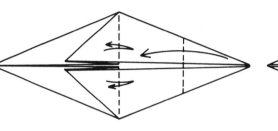

1. Fold a rabbit ear from the top half, and another from the bottom half.

2. Enlarged view. (This basic fold is called the Fish Base.) Fold over and unfold the small flaps in the middle. Fold the right point in to the center.

3. Fold the point back to the right. Note the right-angle symbol on the flap —the valley fold makes a right angle with the lower edge of the model. This means that the edges will line up after folding.

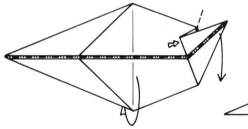

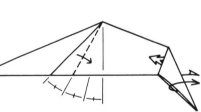

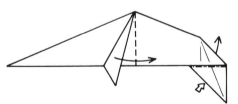

4. Mountain-fold the bottom half of the paper. At the same time, swing the right point downward and pinch it in half.

5. Fold the edge of the small flap one-third of the way over to the right. On the point at the far right (the tail), pull the raw edge of the paper to the right and release the trapped paper that is tucked inside the crimp. Repeat both steps behind.

6. Fold the flap in the middle (the fin) over to the right; repeat behind. Reverse-fold the tail upward.

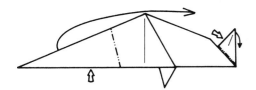 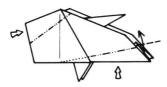 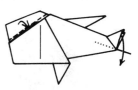

7. Reverse-fold the long point at the left to the right. Reverse-fold the tail into the inside of the model.

8. Reverse-fold the near side only at the left (the head). Reverse-fold the long edge along the bottom. Note that the reverse fold does not entirely clear the pair of points at the tail. This is intentional. Keep the layers of the double point together and treat them as one layer.

9. Tuck the remaining layer of the head into the pocket formed by the reverse fold of step 8. Swing the point inside the tail downward.

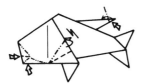

10. Reverse-fold the tip of the fin on the back. Pleat the fin along the side; repeat behind. Dent the front of the head to make a mouth and to make the head slightly three-dimensional.

11. The finished Fish.

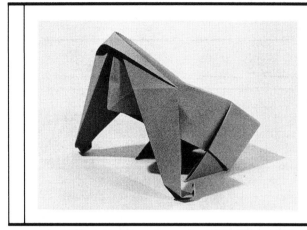

GORILLA

Use a square the same color on both sides. If the paper is colored on one side only, begin with the white side up for a colored model. Crease the paper in half horizontally.

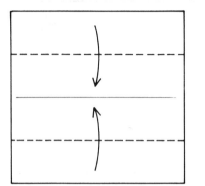

1. Fold the top and bottom edges to the center line.

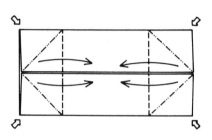

2. Squash-fold all four corners. The next two steps show how to do this easily.

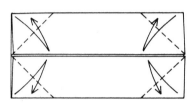

3. First fold in the four corners so that the raw edges of the ends lie along the horizontal center line. Crease and unfold.

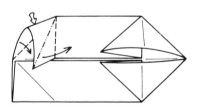

4. Then, beginning with the upper left corner, push down the top edge and bring the loose corner at the center line in toward the middle of the square, mountain-folding this corner in half. This is shown just beginning at the upper left; in progress at the upper right; and completed at the lower right. Do this to all four corners.

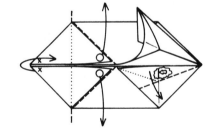

5. On the left, pull the two corners near the middle toward the top and bottom, respectively, as far as they will go (watch the Xs). The left corner stretches out flat. On the right, fold each raw edge outward from the center line toward the folded outer edge and squash-fold the raw edge. (The top one is shown in progress.)

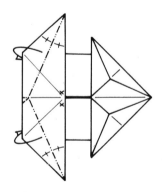

6. Mountain-fold the two corners at the left. The top and bottom points will be folded in half.

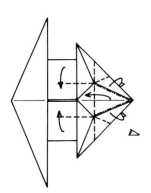

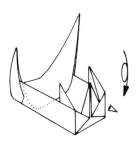

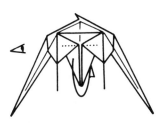

7. Fold the top and bottom sides toward each other so that the paper forms 90-degree angles to the central area. At the same time, mountain-fold the edges of the right corner and bring the point toward you so that it, too, forms a 90-degree angle, like a box.

8. Turn the model over from top to bottom.

9. This is a view of the rear of the Gorilla from the vantage point shown in step 8. For a stronger assembly, separate the layers of the middle point and wrap a single layer around to the inside on each side. The rear will still look the same, but if only one side of the paper is colored, the point will now be colored also. Mountain-fold the middle point into the interior of the model. This locks the rear of the Gorilla together.

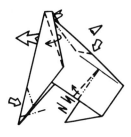

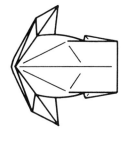

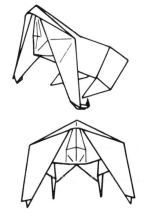

10. Side view from the vantage point shown in step 9. At the end of each arm (at the bottom left) make an inside reverse fold and then an outside reverse fold to form the hands. Outside-reverse-fold the top of the model. Pull out the single layer from inside the front to form the face. The lower edge of the face should be perpendicular to the rear edge of the arm on each side. Crimp the haunches forward along the edges of the legs. Push the back inward to shape it.

11. Top view of back.

12. Push in and shape the face with the creases shown.

13. Two views of the finished Gorilla (from the side and front).

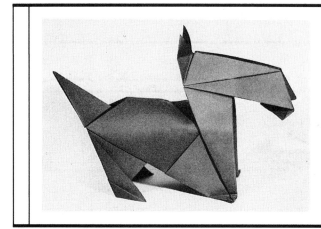

SCOTTIE

Use a square, black on both sides. Crease the paper in half horizontally and then crease the diagonals.

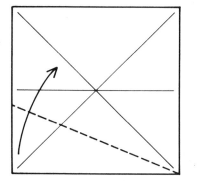

1. Fold the lower left corner up so that the bottom edge of the square will lie along the diagonal.

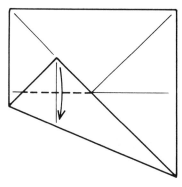

2. Fold the corner down to form a horizontal crease that lies exactly atop the existing center line crease.

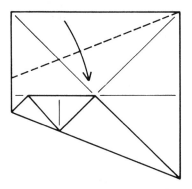

3. Fold the top edge down to match the bottom one.

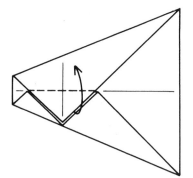

4. Fold one corner back up along a horizontal crease over the center line.

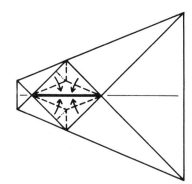

5. Fold two rabbit ears from the corners.

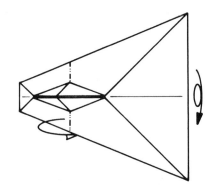

6. Mountain-fold the left end of the model and turn the model over from top to bottom.

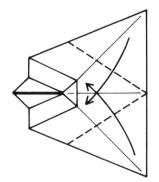

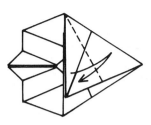

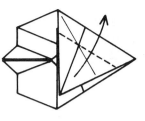

7. Fold the top and bottom right corners toward each other so that their left edges form a straight line. The top flap will overlap the bottom flap.

8. Fold the left edge of the top flap up to the folded edge, crease, and unfold.

9. Fold the flap up along a line that (a) is parallel to the upper right edge, and (b) goes through the intersection of the crease just made.

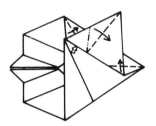

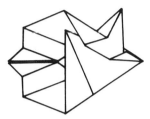

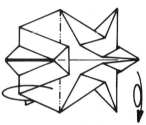

10. Swivel the upper edge of the flap and fold the lower corner of the flap upward along a horizontal line.

11. Repeat steps 8–10 on the lower flap.

12. Mountain-fold the left side of the model and turn the model over from top to bottom.

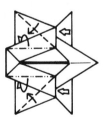

13. Swivel the edges of the left, top and bottom.

14. Mountain-fold the model in half, top to bottom. At the same time, pleat the near layers of paper toward the left; the head, at center left, moves as well.

15. Reverse-fold the left end of the model (the head). Crimp the upper right point (the tail) upward with two reverse folds. Fold the near lower right point to the left; repeat behind.

16. Spread the layers at the muzzle and pull the head upward slightly. Spread the ears apart and fold them down a little. Shape the body with mountain folds as shown, and push in the back. Fold the front feet out to the sides.

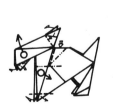

17. Two views of the finished Scottie.

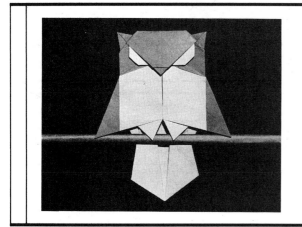

OWL

Use a square colored on one side and white on the other. Begin with the colored side up. Crease the diagonals.

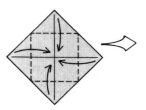

1. Fold all four corners to the center.

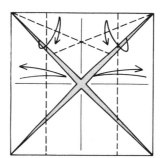

2. Enlarged view. Fold the raw edges of the top flap so that they lie along the top edge of the model; crease, and unfold. Fold the left and right sides in so that they lie along the center line; crease, and unfold.

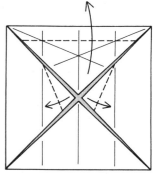

3. Fold the top flap upward; the crease goes through the intersections of the creases made in step 2. Fold the upper edges of the side flaps down so that they lie along the creases made in step 2.

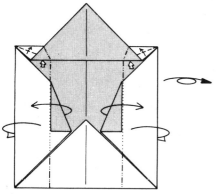

4. Mountain-fold the sides so that they meet at the center line. The middle flaps swing out to the sides, and the raw edges near the left and right upper corners move up to lie along the top folded edge. Turn the paper over from side to side (the next step shows the result).

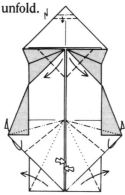

5. Pleat the tip of the top corner. Fold the two bi-colored corners at the top down and outward for the eyes. Swivel the bottom corners outward and tuck the extra paper up behind the side flaps (the wings).

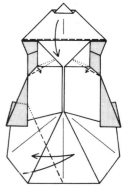

6. Fold the top flap down. Fold the raw edges behind the white triangles (the eyes) down, extending the folds to the tips of the triangles (along the X-ray line; see step 7 for details). Crease the bottom left side through all layers where shown.

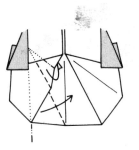

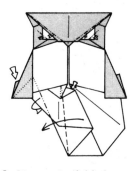

7. Detail of the folds behind the left eye, now raised. Fold the upper part of the raw edge to meet the folded edge as the corner is brought back down.

8. Using the crease made in step 6 as a guide, swivel the left side of the bottom of the model over to the right as shown.

9. Mountain-fold the narrow triangles extending from the ears to the beak. Mountain-fold the tips of the white triangles (the eyes). Make a swivel fold on the left side of the model under and behind the wing (see steps 10–11 for a view of this from the other side). Fold back to the left the white flap that crosses the center line, forming a reverse fold where it goes under the foot (in the center of the model).

10. This is how the swivel fold of the wing looks from the back.

11. Finished swivel fold.

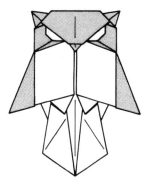

12. (Front view, again.) Pleat the top corners of the head to form ear tufts. Mountain-fold the bottom edge of the left wing. Repeat steps 6–9 on the bottom of the right side.

13. The finished Owl. Make the vertical center crease a slight mountain crease on the back to give the body depth and to keep the center edges at the front close together. The Owl will perch on a thin horizontal edge, such as a glass, branch, or rod.

GOOSE

Use a square the same color on both sides. If the paper is colored on one side only, begin with the white side up for a predominantly colored model. Crease the paper in half vertically and horizontally and crease the diagonals.

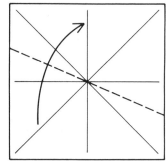

1. Fold the paper in half so that the horizontal crease lies on top of the diagonal crease and the fold runs through the middle of the paper.

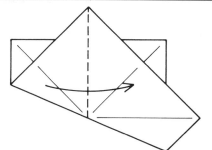

2. Fold the left side over to the right on vertical existing creases.

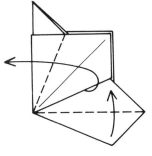

3. Fold the flap back to the left so that its corner lines up with the top corner. Fold the bottom edge up on an existing crease.

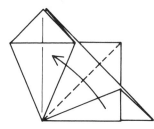

4. Fold the right flap up on an existing crease.

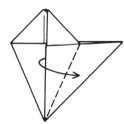

5. Fold the flap back to the right so that its edge lines up with the outer folded edge.

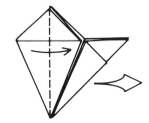

6. Fold the left edge over.

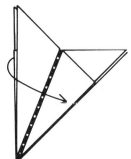

7. Enlarged view. Fold the model in half, left to right.

8. Fold one of the four flaps over to the left; the fold is at right angles to the raw edges of the paper, so that the top edge of the model forms a straight line as in step 9.

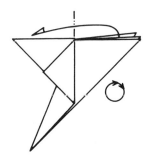

9. Repeat step 8 on the farthest flap. Rotate the model one-eighth turn, so that the long edge lies along the bottom.

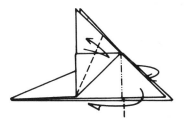 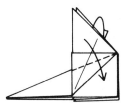 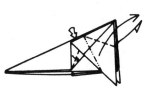

10. Fold the near vertical flap to the right so that its left edge lines up with the diagonal folded edge and unfold; repeat behind. Mountain-fold the near flap at the right into the inside of the model; repeat behind.

11. Fold the near flap down along a crease that aligns with the edge of the middle layers behind it; repeat behind, symmetrically.

12. Swivel the near flap upward, using the creases made in step 10 as a guide; repeat behind.

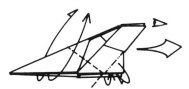 

13. Mountain-fold the corner at the bottom right to the inside, in line with the slanted raw edge above it; repeat behind. Outside-reverse-fold the left point so that edges touch the corner of the long triangle on each side (see step 16).

14. Enlarged view from the rear. Outside-reverse-fold the head. Crimp the tail down . . .

15. . . . and shift the wings upward, as shown in this end-on view.

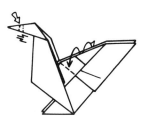

16. Form the beak with two reverse folds. Spread the wings.

17. The finished Goose. For additional shaping, gently press in the back of the neck.

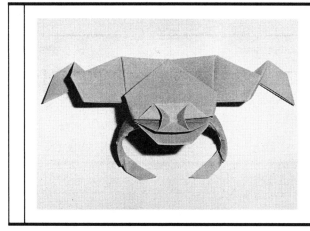

FROG

Use a square of thin artist's paper the same color on both sides—the paper should contain sizing—or use paper-backed foil. If foil is used, begin with the white side up for a colored model. Crease the paper into eighths both vertically and horizontally and crease the diagonals.

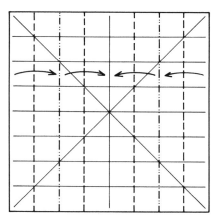

1. Pleat the paper vertically in eighths from each side to the middle.

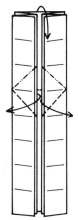

2. Spread the layers as shown and bring the top of the model down.

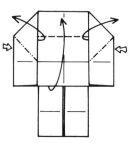

3. Spread the edges shown and lift the flap upward again.

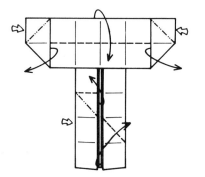

4. Spread the raw edges again and fold the top raw edge downward. Squash-fold the right side at the bottom of the model, pulling up all layers.

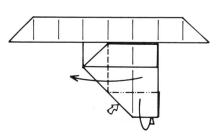

5. Swing the bottom flap over to the left and squash-fold the bottom of it.

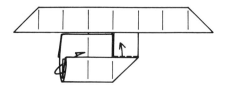

6. Pull the two layers upward from the interior of the bottom flap.

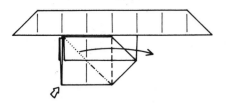

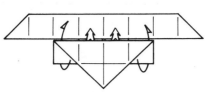

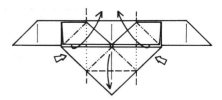

7. Squash-fold the bottom flap.

8. Grasp the left central corner and twist it away from you as shown; bring it all the way to the top and flatten. Repeat on the right.

9. Swing the two corners upward; simultaneously, pull the middle of the raw edge downward and the sides inward along valley folds (indicated by X-ray lines).

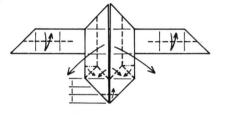

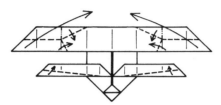

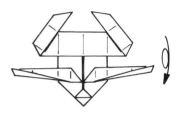

10. Crease the two long horizontal flaps in half. Make two long rabbit ears from the two vertical flaps. Fold one-third of the bottom tip upward (near flap only).

11. Fold rabbit ears from the horizontal flaps at the top, using the indicated reference points and the creases made in step 10. Fold the long lower edges of the lower pair of flaps upward so that they just cross the corners of the ends.

12. Turn the paper over from top to bottom.

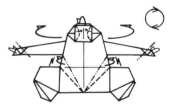

15. Curve the forelegs away from you and fold the tips away and upward to form feet. Raise the edges of the eyes to open and round them (the back edge of the head will rise also). Pleat the body as shown and adjust the hind legs so that the feet and rump touch the ground.

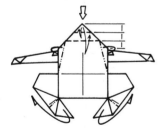

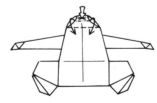

13. Crease the near point at the top of the model into thirds as shown. Mountain-fold the side corners of the body. Mountain-fold the bottom flaps (the legs) outward so that the tips touch the outer corners.

14. Spread the layers of the near point and pull the near layer on each side downward, folding on the lower crease made in step 13; at the same time, press on the tip so that it flattens into a square that is defined by the upper crease made in step 13. This maneuver is sometimes called a "lover's knot" or a "spread sink."

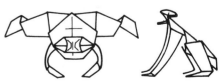

16. Two views of the finished Frog.

LION

Use a square the same color on both sides. If the paper is colored on one side only, begin with the white side up for a colored model. Crease the paper in half horizontally and crease the diagonals.

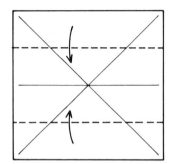

1. Fold the top and bottom edges inward to the horizontal crease.

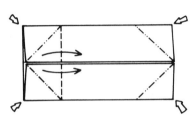

2. Squash-fold the two corners at the left (see Gorilla, page 36, for an example). Reverse-fold the two at the right.

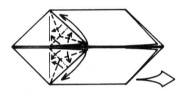

3. Fold a rabbit ear from each of the two flaps at the left.

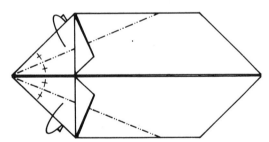

4. Enlarged view. Mountain-fold the upper and lower edges on the left.

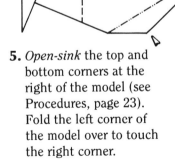

5. *Open-sink* the top and bottom corners at the right of the model (see Procedures, page 23). Fold the left corner of the model over to touch the right corner.

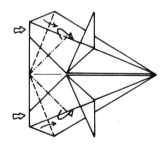

6. Swivel in the left edges.

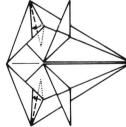

7. Fold edge to edge, reverse-folding beneath the near layers (X-ray lines).

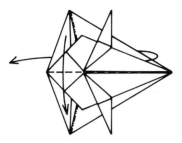

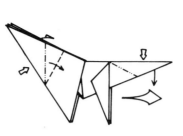

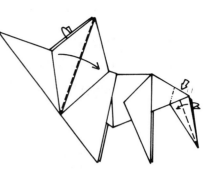

8. Bring the large flap on the far side back to the left with the mountain folds shown; simultaneously fold the entire model in half, top to bottom.

9. Squash-fold the near and far flaps at the left with the interior layers pushed to one side. Reverse-fold the point at the right (the tail).

10. Enlarged view. Fold the left half of the flap to the right. Narrow the tail with a reverse fold at its base. Repeat behind.

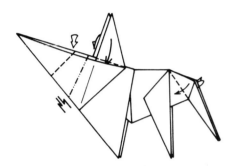

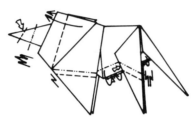

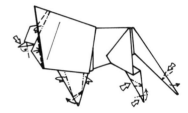

11. Tuck the long points (the ears) down inside. Crimp the left point (the muzzle) with reverse folds. Fold the tail down on each side, around itself.

12. Reverse-fold the muzzle in and out. Fold the ears to the left. Pleat the foreleg. Mountain-fold the belly inside, along with the area under the tail. Crimp the hind leg. Repeat everything behind.

13. Reverse-fold the lower jaw. Pleat each ear and tuck it into the pocket formed by the reverse fold of step 11. Crimp the bottom of the foreleg to form a paw and narrow the leg, with swivel folds at the top inside (see step 15). Crimp and reverse-fold the hind leg. Repeat behind. Crimp the tip of the tail upward.

14. Reverse-fold the tip of the nose; repeat behind.

15. This is an interior view of the swivel folds that narrow the foreleg.

16. Pull the layers out from the inside of the tip of the tail to form a tuft.

17. The finished Lion.

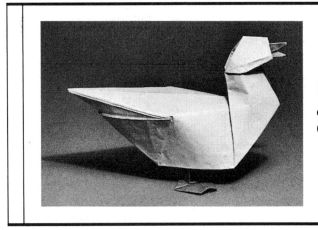

DUCK

Use a square, orange on one side and white on the other. Begin with the orange side up. Crease the diagonals.

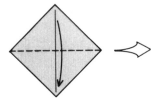

1. Fold the top corner down to the bottom corner.

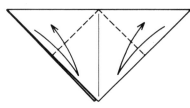

2. Enlarged view. Fold each side corner down to the bottom corner, crease, and unfold.

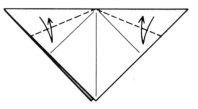

3. Fold the top edge on the left and right down to the creases just made, crease, and unfold.

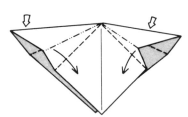

4. Squash-fold each side corner as shown (the left side is just starting; the right side is shown in progress). Make sure that the center line of each squashed flap is aligned with the folded edge behind it.

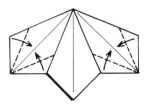

5. Fold the outer raw edges of each squash fold so that they lie along the diagonal center creases.

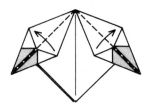

6. Fold the inner edges to the outer edges, in effect closing up the squash folds.

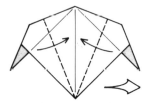

7. Fold the sides in so that the lower raw edges of the paper meet along the center line.

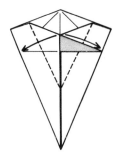

8. Enlarged view. Fold each of the colored points toward the outer edge so that the corner of the white part touches the edge and the crease goes through the upper corner of the white flap.

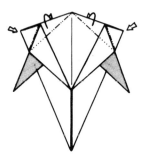

9. Swivel by mountain-folding, pulling the left and right upper corners to the rear; press the corners flat (see step 11 for the result).

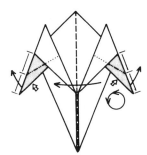

10. Reverse-fold the colored points out to the sides. Fold the paper in half vertically, right to left, and rotate a quarter-turn counterclockwise.

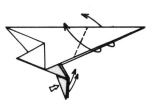

11. Reverse-fold the colored points (the feet) and outside-reverse-fold the white point at the right (the neck).

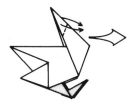

12. Outside-reverse-fold the neck to form a head.

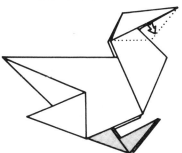

13. Enlarged view. Pull out a single layer of paper from each side of the head.

14. This cut-away view shows how the hidden flap remains folded.

15. Form a beak with two reverse folds, folding both the outer (white) flap and the inner (colored) flap together as one.

16. Reverse-fold the bottom front corner of the head; repeat behind.

17. Fold the bottom edge of the beak upward to change its color and narrow it. Mountain-fold the bottom corner of the head. Repeat behind.

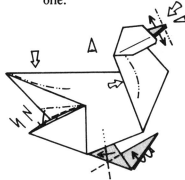

18. Open the beak and blunt the tips with a reverse fold on the upper beak and a sink on the lower beak, and spread apart the upper and lower beak. Open out the body by flattening the top edge of the back. Crimp the tail on each side and tuck the resulting flap into the pocket shown at the top of the wing. Open out the feet and turn them away from each other by folding the legs backward. Gently press in the back of the neck to shape it.

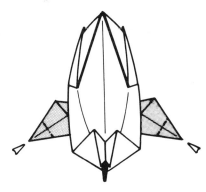

19. Top view. Sink the tips of the feet.

20. Two views of the finished Duck.

SEA TURTLE

Use a square colored on one side and white on the other. Begin with the white side up for a colored shell. Crease the paper in half vertically and horizontally and crease the diagonals. Rotate the paper to the position shown here.

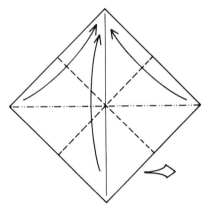

1. Fold a Preliminary Fold with the four corners of the square at the top.

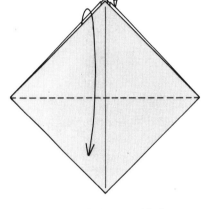

2. Enlarged view. Fold the near top corner down to the bottom and the far top corner down behind.

3. Fold the near left corner in to the middle of the model; repeat behind.

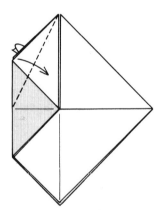

4. Fold the near upper left edge to the right along a crease that connects the top of the model with the middle of the left edge; repeat behind.

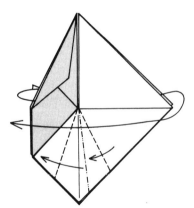

5. Fold the near right corner over to the left, *incorporating* the asymmetrical *reverse fold* in the single layer at the bottom (see Procedures, page 18). Repeat on the far side, so that the model ends up symmetrical.

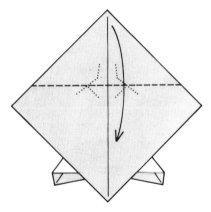

6. Fold down one corner; the crease line goes through the intersections of the hidden edges indicated by the X-ray lines.

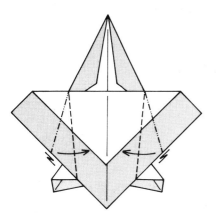

7. Pleat the sides inward so that the short outer edge on each side is vertical.

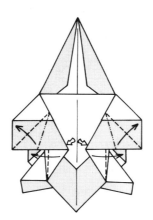

8. Swivel the sides.

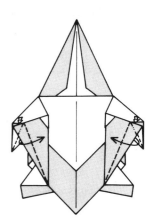

9. Swivel again.

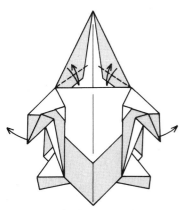

10. Crease the angle bisectors at the top of the model by bringing each outer edge of the top point down to the horizontal edge, creasing, and unfolding. Unfold the sides to step 7.

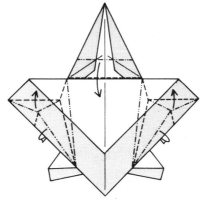

11. Reassemble the sides of the model, using existing creases. Some of the creases, however, will have to be inverted (changing mountain into valley folds or vice versa). Pleat the top point downward (note the reference points).

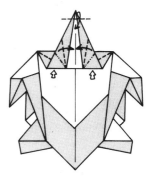

12. Swivel the side corners of the top point (the head). Fold the tip down.

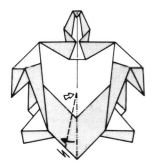

13. Pleat the lower part of the model (the shell). The back of the shell will curve upward and will no longer lie flat.

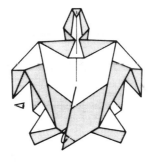

14. Mountain-fold the tiny point at the bottom of the shell into the interior of the shell; this locks it together.

15. Side view. The legs are not shown in steps 15–16. Spread the layers on the underside of the head and pull out the bottom of the shell to make it three-dimensional . . .

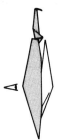

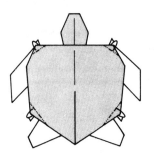

16. . . . like this.

17. Top view. Mountain-fold the corners of the shell to round them.

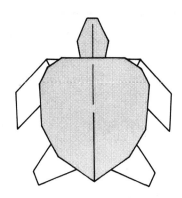

18. The finished Sea Turtle.

ROADRUNNER

Use a square of paper-backed foil. Begin with the white side up for a colored model. Crease the paper in half vertically and horizontally and crease the diagonals. Rotate the paper to the position shown here.

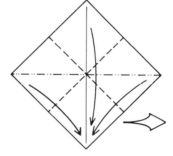

1. Fold a Preliminary Fold.

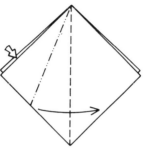

2. Enlarged view. Squash-fold the near left flap.

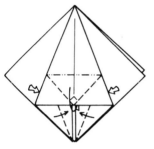

3. *Inside-petal-fold* the squashed flap (see Procedures, page 22).

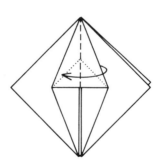

4. Fold the right side of the squashed flap to the left.

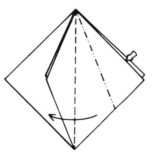

5. Repeat steps 2–4 on the right.

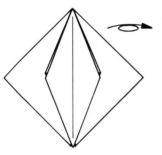

6. Turn the paper over from side to side.

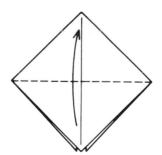

7. Fold a single layer up as far as it will go.

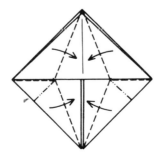

8. Fold a rabbit ear from each of the side corners.

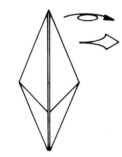

9. Turn the paper over from side to side.

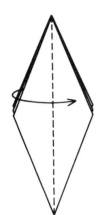

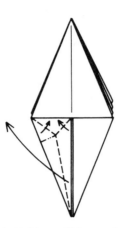

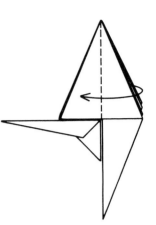

10. Enlarged view. Fold one flap from the left to the right.

11. Fold a rabbit ear from the lower left point.

12. Fold two flaps from the right back to the left.

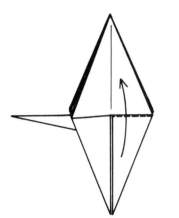

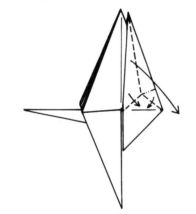

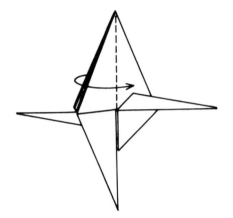

13. Fold the lower right point up as far as it will go.

14. Fold a rabbit ear from this point.

15. Fold a single flap from the left back to the right.

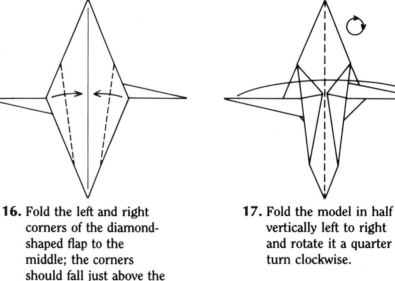

16. Fold the left and right corners of the diamond-shaped flap to the middle; the corners should fall just above the center of the diamond and the folds should not reach the bottom point.

17. Fold the model in half vertically left to right and rotate it a quarter turn clockwise.

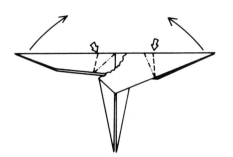

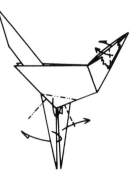

18. Crimp the left flap (the tail) and the right flap (the head) upward with reverse folds. The tail crimp is shown with the wing cut away.

19. Mountain-fold the bottom left point to the left and valley-fold the bottom right point to the right. Mountain-fold the lower corner of the body inside; repeat behind. The head is shown with a cut-away view; outside-reverse-fold the inner point backward so that its rear edge is perpendicular to the back of the neck.

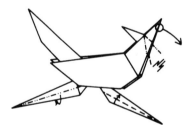

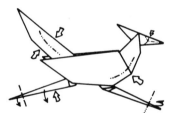

20. Mountain-fold the left leg behind to narrow it; valley-fold the right leg similarly. Crimp the head downward.

21. Push in the top edge of the tail and the front of the body to make them three-dimensional. Bend the left leg slightly forward about a third of the way down and fold the tips of both legs out away from each other to make feet.

22. The finished Roadrunner. If very carefully adjusted and balanced, the model will stand by itself.

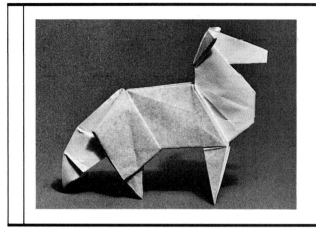

COLLIE

Use a square, brown on one side and white on the other. Begin with the brown side up. Crease the diagonals and the oblique angle bisectors on the left and right.

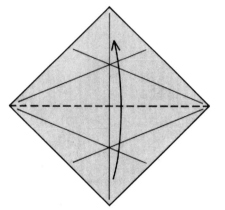

1. Fold the bottom up to the top of the square.

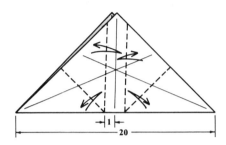

2. Make vertical valley folds on each side of the center line, spaced ¹⁄₂₀ of the total width from the center. Crease the bisectors of the angles made by those valley folds with the bottom folded edge.

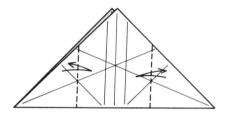

3. Crease a vertical valley fold on each side through the intersection of the two creases shown.

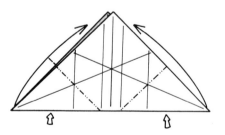

4. Reverse-fold the left and right creases on existing creases.

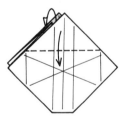

5. Fold one layer down. Note that the valley fold connects the points where the creases made in step 3 meet the edge of the paper. Repeat behind.

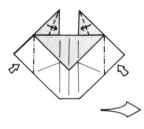

6. Reverse-fold on existing creases; repeat behind.

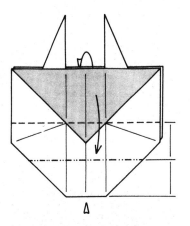

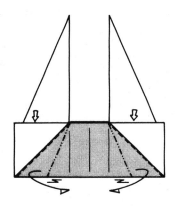

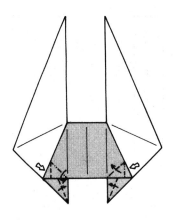

7. Enlarged view. First, open-sink the bottom point up inside the model (note the reference points). Then, fold the large rectangular flaps down in front and behind.

8. The top of the sink and the edges of the valley folds of step 7 should all line up in the middle, as shown here. Pleat the paper as shown (it will be easiest if you flatten out the white part before squashing the colored region); repeat behind.

9. Reverse-fold the left side. Squash-fold the right side (note the differences). Repeat behind.

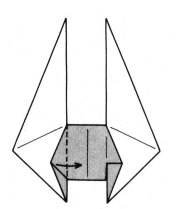

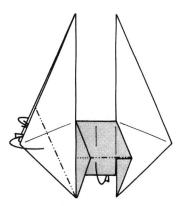

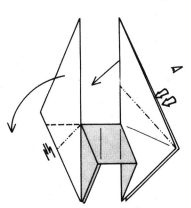

10. Fold the colored flap at the left to the right; repeat behind.

11. Mountain-fold the lower left edge as far inside the white flap as possible. Mountain-fold to the inside of the model the colored layer at the bottom. Repeat behind.

12. Crimp the left side downward so that the top edge is horizontal. Double-reverse-fold the right side. To accomplish this, partially open out the paper and reverse-fold the near and far layers side by side.

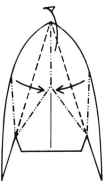

13. This shows the double-reverse fold in progress with the paper partially opened out and all the creases visible. Close the model when done.

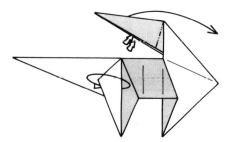

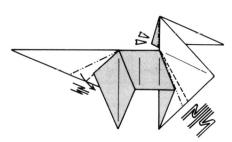

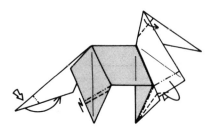

14. Double reverse-fold the point back to the right, in the same manner as in steps 12–13. Wrap the single white layer on the vertical left flap (the hind leg) around to the far side of the flap; repeat behind.

15. Crimp the white flap at the left (the tail) downward. Open-sink the two dark corners at the top right (the back of the head). Crimp the paper at the lower right (the chest), but leave the innermost pair of layers uncrimped.

16. Reverse-fold the tip of the tail. Pleat the hind leg. Mountain-fold and pleat the foreleg. Fold the ear forward. Repeat behind.

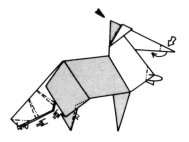

17. This shows an interior view of the Collie's completed left foreleg.

18. Mountain-fold the end of the tail inside; repeat behind. Crimp the tail. Mountain-fold the front edge of the hind leg, and swivel to form a collar behind the pleats (see step 19). *Closed-sink* the colored point at the top of the head (this is very difficult to do neatly— see Procedures, page 24). Mountain-fold the chest inside; repeat behind. Reverse-fold the nose.

19. This shows an interior view of the Collie's completed left hind leg.

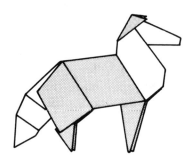

20. The finished Collie.

KANGAROO

Use a square of thin paper at least ten inches on a side; both sides should be the same color. Crease the paper in half vertically and horizontally and crease the diagonals.

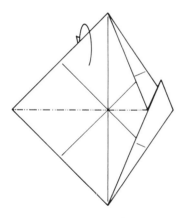

1. Fold the four corners behind to the center.

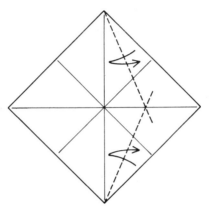

2. Fold the upper and lower right edges to the vertical crease line, crease, and unfold.

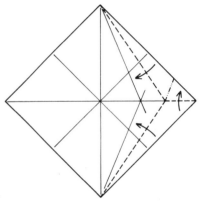

3. Fold a rabbit ear from the right corner, bringing the upper and lower right edges to the crease lines just made.

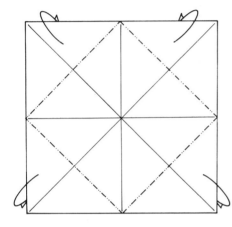

4. Mountain-fold the top half of the model.

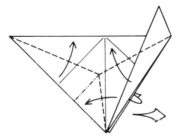

5. Fold a rabbit ear from the near flap; repeat behind.

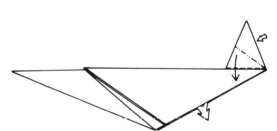

6. Enlarged view. Squash-fold the top right corner. Pull the loose paper out from the bottom of the model (two layers).

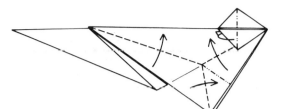

7. Mountain-fold the
squash-folded corner into
the interior of the model.
Fold a rabbit ear from
the near layer just pulled
out; repeat behind on the
far layer.

8. Squash-fold the rabbit
ear flap upward; repeat
behind. Fold the near
flap on the right point
upward.

9. Petal-fold the small
squashed flap downward;
repeat behind. Fold the
large flap to the right,
crease, and unfold;
repeat behind.

10. Squash-fold the indicated
flap asymmetrically. The
right corner of the
squash touches the top
corner of the petal fold
made in step 9. Repeat
behind.

11. Petal-fold the flap, but
don't flatten it out
entirely.

12. Before flattening the
petal fold, add a valley
fold extending from the
bottom right to the
upper left corner under
the near layer and swivel
the bottom point to the
right. Then flatten it out.
Repeat steps 11–12
behind.

13. Swivel the lower right
layers of the large flap
(the hind leg) away from
you, bringing the edges
of the bottom point
together. Swivel the tip
of the smaller right point
(the foreleg) to the left,
similarly to step 12.

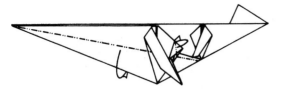 

14. Mountain-fold the bottom left edge of the model into the interior. Mountain-fold the right corner of the hind leg. Repeat behind.

15. Mountain-fold the bottom right edge of the model inside; repeat behind.

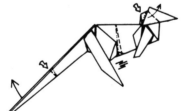

16. Reverse-fold the long left point (the tail) downward at the angle shown. Fold down the near flap at the right and fold down the far flap behind.

17. Fold the top edge of the tail forward and down, tucking it behind the layers of the hind leg; repeat behind. Mountain-fold the tiny corner at the top of the hind legs; repeat behind. Crimp the head upward with two reverse folds.

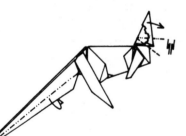

18. Mountain-fold the bottom edge of the tail inside; repeat behind. Crimp the head downward, folding only the inner layers.

19. Crimp the tail upward with two reverse folds. Crimp the body. Swing the flap on the head upward, simultaneously flattening the left corner into a collar; repeat behind.

20. Dent the top of the head with a reverse fold. Swivel the front of the ear behind; repeat behind.

21. Blunt the nose with a reverse fold.

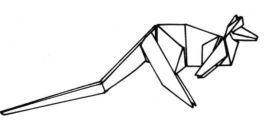

22. The finished Kangaroo.

SQUIRREL

Use a square the same color on both sides. If the paper is colored on one side only, begin with the white side up for a predominantly colored model. Crease the paper in half along one diagonal.

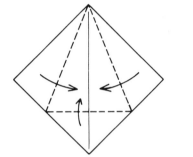

1. Fold the upper edges in to the center line and fold the lower corner up to cover them.

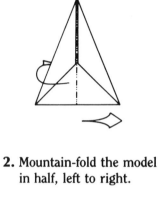

2. Mountain-fold the model in half, left to right.

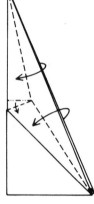

3. Enlarged view. Fold a rabbit ear from the top portion of the model, folding all the layers together as one.

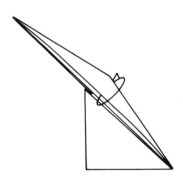

4. Wrap a single layer from front to back.

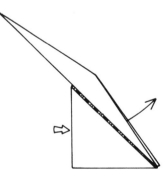

5. Reverse-fold the bottom corner.

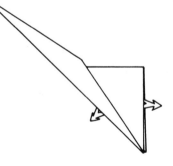

6. Pull the two loose corners out from the bottom left and the single loose corner out from the right.

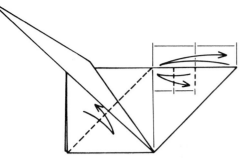

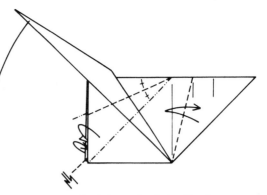

7. Crease through all layers as shown. Fold and unfold the left square area along the diagonal. Fold in half the upper edge of the right flap and make a small crease. Then fold this small crease to the tip of the center line and make another small crease.

8. Crimp the left side down so that the horizontal edge lines up with the mountain fold; the valley fold is the bisector. Fold and unfold the right, connecting the two points shown.

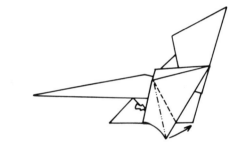

9. Make two outside reverse folds back and forth, using the crease made in step 8.

10. Swivel the near right lower corner upward along a crease that makes a right angle with the raw edge. The paper will not lie flat.

11. Squash the raised corner over to the right so that it lies a little below the lower right corner; flatten it into the position shown in step 12.

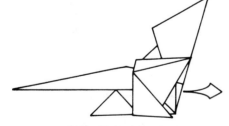

12. Repeat steps 10–11 behind to match.

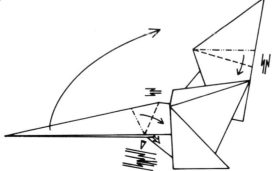

13. Enlarged view. Crimp the top corner (the head) down. Note the point-of-view symbol at the base of the tail. You must separate the interior layers from the crimp and reverse the creases of the far layer to match the near one so that they look like this. Crimp the left point (the tail) upward.

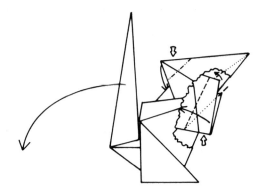

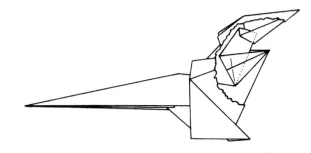

14. Swing the tail back downward. Reverse-fold the back of the head into the neck as far as possible. The cut-away view shows the far layers of the model from the inside. Squash-fold the middle corner at the right upward, simultaneously narrowing the head. Repeat on the near layers, which are cut away in this view.

15. Like this.

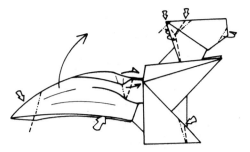

16. Pull the raw edges of the tail out from the bottom and push up the middle folded edge to fluff it out. Reverse-fold the tip of the nose. Swivel the underside of the foreleg; repeat behind. Pull out the corner of the head.

17. Crimp the tail upward on existing creases, flattening the folded edge inside; push its tip down slightly. Crimp the top of the head to form an ear, using an existing crease; note that the crimp does not go to the edges of the ear, which are cupped slightly forward. Narrow the face with a mountain fold. Crimp the foot. Repeat behind.

18. View of the tail from the rear.

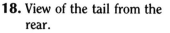

19. The finished Squirrel.

SKUNK

Use a square, black on one side, white on the other. Begin with the white side up. Crease the diagonals. You will need a ruler to measure several distances on this model. All dimensions are in the same units (centimeters, for example). The square is twenty-three units on a side.

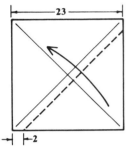

1. Fold the lower right corner up to the upper left. The valley fold intersects the side of the square 2 units in from the corner.

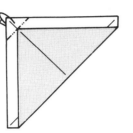

2. Mountain-fold the upper left corner. The mountain fold just touches the tip of the dark corner.

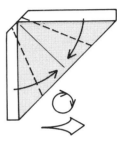

3. Fold the raw edges in to the diagonal crease. Rotate the model a quarter turn clockwise.

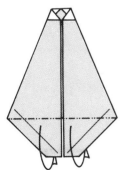

4. Enlarged view. Mountain-fold the two bottom flaps behind the model.

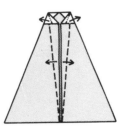

5. Fold outward the long raw edges along the center line. Squash outward the little pockets at the top.

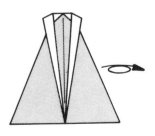

6. Turn the model over from side to side.

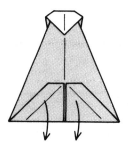

7. Fold the two flaps down again.

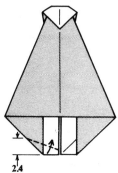

8. Fold as shown. The valley fold intersects the left edge 2.4 units up, and when the fold is complete, its top edge is horizontal.

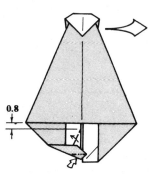

9. Swivel the edge of the flap; the valley fold begins 0.8 units down from the horizontal folded edge.

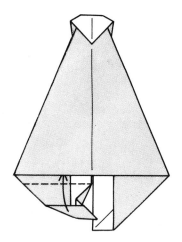

10. Enlarged view. Tuck the flap inside the model.

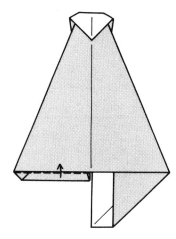

11. Fold the narrow protruding layers up over the folded edge. Repeat steps 8–11 on the right.

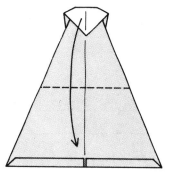

12. Fold the model in half from top to bottom.

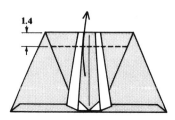

13. Fold the near flap up again, 1.4 units down from the top.

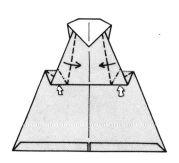

14. Swivel the sides.

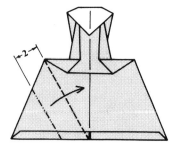

15. Pleat the left side of the model. The mountain fold is parallel to and 2 units away from the valley fold.

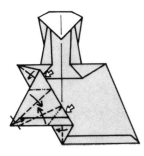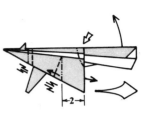

16. Swivel. Repeat steps 15–16 on the right.

17. Fold the model in half from left to right. Rotate it a quarter turn clockwise.

18. Crimp the point at the left (the head). Crimp the haunches. Push in the top of the body at the base of the tail, and lift the tail up. These last two folds will make the body three-dimensional.

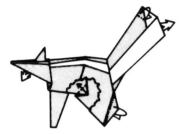

19. Pull the narrow flap out from inside the head. The cut-away view shows the far side from the inside of the model; fold the corner inside the haunches to lock the pleat. Mountain-fold the rear corner along the folded edge of the hind leg. Repeat everything on the other side. Mountain-fold the dark corner at the top of the tail inside and pull the paper out from inside the tip of the tail.

20. Mountain-fold the front corner of the lower jaw. Pinch the feet to shape them. Repeat behind. Crimp the tail downward.

21. Enlarged view of the head. The tip of the nose consists of three interlocking points. Spread the points slightly; mountain-fold the two lower ones into the interior of the head, and valley-fold the middle one back over the nose. Mountain-fold the narrow white edge on each side of the head inside to hide it.

22. Pleat the ears and reverse-fold their tips.

23. Three views of the finished Skunk.

PANDA

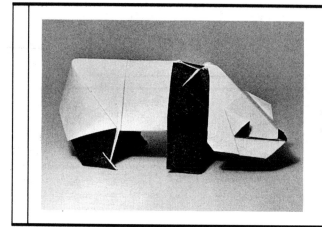

Use a square, black on one side and white on the other. Begin with the white side up. Crease the diagonals.

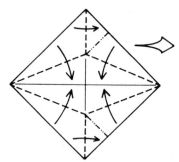

1. Fold the top and bottom triangles into rabbit ears to make a Fish Base (see Fish, page 34).

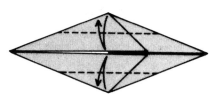

2. Enlarged view. Fold the top and bottom corners in to the center and unfold.

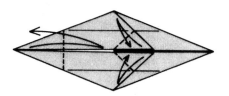

3. Fold the left corner in to the center and unfold. Fold the tips of the rabbit ear flaps out to the top and bottom corners and unfold.

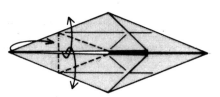

4. Spread apart the raw edges along the center line; simultaneously bring the left corner over to the center of the model.

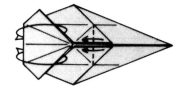

5. Turn the flap on the left inside out, opening the model to make it easier. Fold the tips of the rabbit ear flaps to the center.

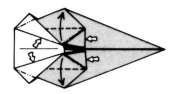

6. Bring the near colored layer of the upper half of the model all the way to the top; the paper will swivel as indicated by the push arrows. Flatten into the configuration of step 7. Repeat on the lower half.

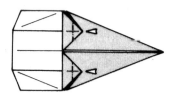

7. Open-sink the corners halfway.

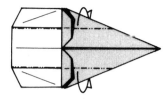

8. Mountain-fold the edges of the far flap, top and bottom. Do not fold the near layers on the left.

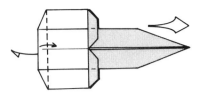

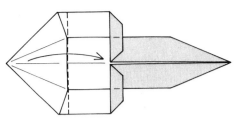

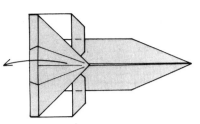

9. Fold the left edge to the right, forming a crease that connects the top and bottom corners. Allow the single-layer flap on the far side to swing out from behind to the left.

10. Enlarged view. Fold the entire left assembly to the right along its vertical folded edge.

11. Swing the large triangular flap to the left and allow the narrow flap behind it (from step 9) to swing out to the right.

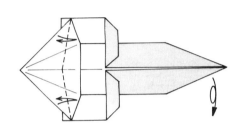

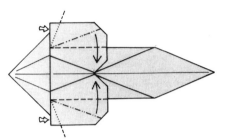

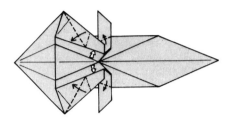

12. Crease the angle bisectors. Turn the model over from top to bottom.

13. Swivel the top and bottom inward.

14. Swivel again.

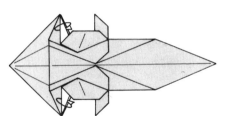

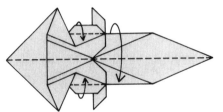

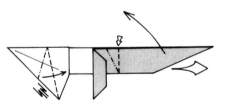

15. Lift the white flaps and tuck them into the pockets as shown.

16. Fold in the short small flaps at top and bottom so that the creases line up with the edges behind. Fold the entire model in half lengthwise from top to bottom.

17. Crimp symmetrically the left end of the model (the tail). Crimp upward the right end (the head) with two reverse folds.

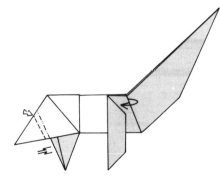

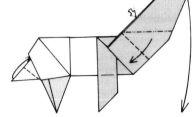

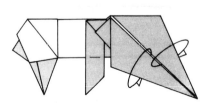

18. Enlarged view. Crimp the tail. Pull out one layer of paper on each side at the base of the neck and reposition as shown in step 19.

19. Outside-reverse-fold the tail into the model as far as possible. Squash-fold the head downward.

20. Wrap the layers from the near side of the head around to the far side. Partially opening the model makes this easier.

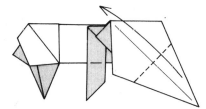

21. Fold the tip of the head up to the left a little past the top.

22. Detail of the head. Spread the raw edges and bring the tip back down to the center of the folded edge in the same manner as in step 4.

23. Squash-fold the side corners to make eyes, and fold the bottom tip up for the nose.

 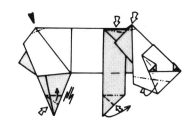

24. Mountain-fold the upper half of the head.

25. Closed-sink the rump. Push in the top of the neck and head. Mountain-fold the bottom edges of the head into the interior of the model. Crimp the front and rear feet.

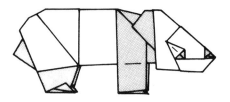

26. The finished Panda.

FOX

Use a square of paper-backed foil. Begin with the white side up for a colored model. Crease the paper in half horizontally.

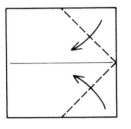

1. Fold the upper and lower halves of the right edge so that they lie along the horizontal crease.

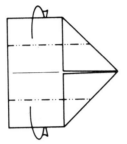

2. Mountain-fold the top and bottom edges so that they meet along the horizontal center crease.

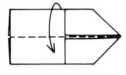

3. Fold the model in half horizontally.

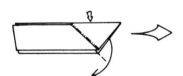

4. Reverse-fold the right corner of the model downward, aligning the crease line exactly with the folded edges.

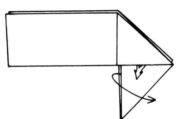

5. Enlarged view. Pull the loose paper out where shown; repeat behind.

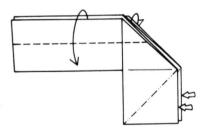

6. Fold a single raw edge down to the bottom horizontal edge; repeat behind. Reverse-fold the near lower right corner; repeat behind.

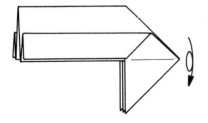

7. Turn the paper over from top to bottom.

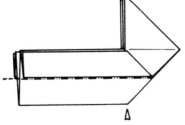

8. Open-sink the bottom layers upward to be even with the other layers.

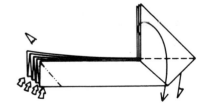

9. Reverse-fold all of the corners at the left. Fold the near flap at the right down; repeat behind.

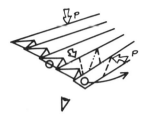

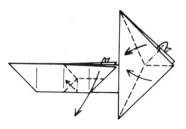

10. This shows the left side from above, partially opened out. Grasp the near corner and the middle corner and stretch them apart from each other while pinching where the arrows marked P are shown. Flatten out the paper.

11. This shows the fold from the underside, completed. Repeat behind.

12. Fold a rabbit ear from the near left flap; repeat behind. Fold a rabbit ear from the near triangle at the right; repeat behind.

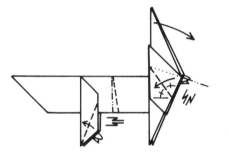

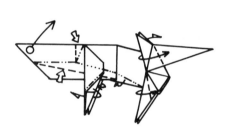

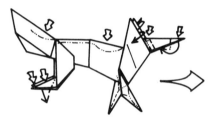

13. Fold the lower edge of the near lower left flap (the hind leg) up to the left edge; repeat behind. Crimp the body. Crimp the right side; note the reference points for the valley fold. As the short points (the ears) swing leftward, the long point (the head) will swing down.

14. Crimp the top half of the left end (the tail) at the rear of the hind leg; at the same time, on each side, mountain-fold the lower half of the tail, extending the mountain fold to the foreleg. Finish the tail by forming, both in front and in back, the long valley fold that is near the bottom. Mountain-fold the hind leg to the left along the folded edge; repeat behind. Fold the left edge of the near foreleg to the folded edge (do not repeat behind). Fold the ears to the right.

15. Shape the body with soft mountain folds. Reverse-fold the hind legs downward. Crimp the face and spread the ears. Reverse-fold the tip of the nose. Pinch the forelegs.

16. Just inside the forelegs is a pleat; lock it by folding the corner up, as shown.

17. The finished Fox. The fox stands on three legs with one foreleg raised.

IRISH SETTER

Use a rectangle of proportions 8½:11 (thin letter paper will do), the same color on both sides. If the paper is colored on one side only, begin with the white side up for a predominantly colored model. Crease the paper in half vertically and horizontally.

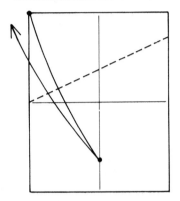

1. Fold the upper left corner down so that the crease runs through the midpoint of the left side and the corner touches the vertical crease. Unfold.

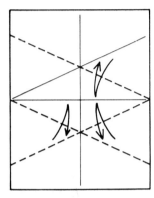

2. Fold and unfold the other three corners similarly.

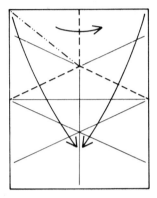

3. Fold a rabbit ear from the upper half of the rectangle, using the creases just made as a guide.

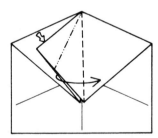

4. Squash-fold the middle flap.

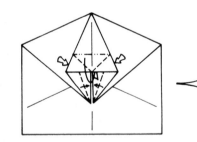

5. Inside-petal-fold the flap.

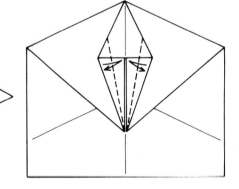

6. Enlarged view. Crease the angle bisectors.

7. Using the crease just made as a guide, petal-fold, raising the horizontal folded edge while folding the sides in.

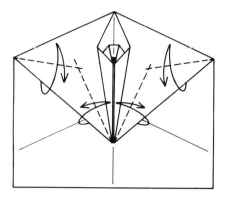 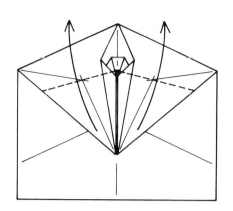 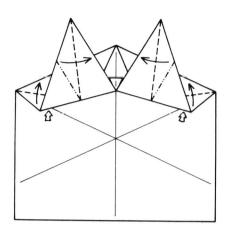

8. Crease the angle bisectors of the triangular flap on the right and left sides of the model; do not crease the far layer.

9. Fold the two near points upward; the creases meet at the center line as far up as possible, and they run through the intersections of the pairs of bisectors made in step 9.

10. Swivel in the sides of the two points, using the creases from step 8 as a guide.

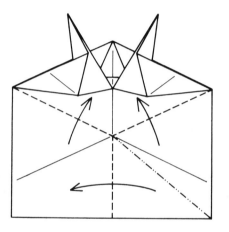 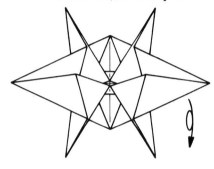 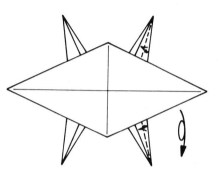

11. Repeat steps 3–10 on the lower half of the rectangle.

12. Turn the paper over from top to bottom.

13. Bring the right edge of the upper right point to the folded edge near the middle, crease, and unfold. Repeat on the lower right point. Turn the model over from top to bottom.

14. Swing the upper and lower right points to the left, allowing the layers to swivel. Adjust the position of the points so that the creases made in step 13 are exactly vertical. Flatten the points in their new positions, making new creases. When properly positioned, the vertical crease on each leg should intersect the crease of the former edge (see step 15).

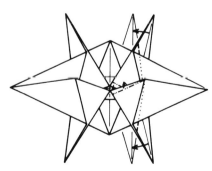

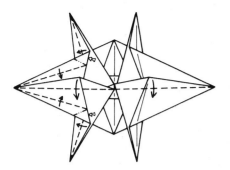

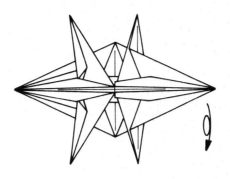

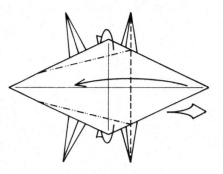

15. Swivel the near layers of the upper and lower left points, extending the folds to the left corner of the model. In the middle of the model, fold the thick central edges downward, being careful to keep the layers and positions of the points in place. Fold the edges behind them upward, in the same manner.

16. Turn the paper over from top to bottom.

17. Fold the right point to the left; the crease runs from the tip of the upper right point to the tip of the lower right point. Mountain-fold the top and bottom corners of the diamond shape as shown.

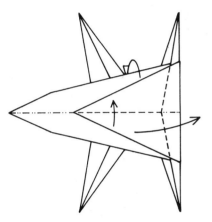

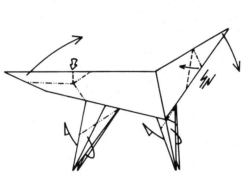

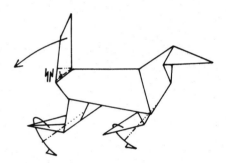

18. Enlarged view. Mountain-fold the model in half, top to bottom, simultaneously forming a rabbit ear from the central flap and swinging it up to the right.

19. Fold the left point (the tail) upward with a double rabbit ear. Mountain-fold the near lower left point (the hind leg) to the left; repeat behind. Mountain-fold the near right lower point (the foreleg) to the left; repeat behind. Crimp the right point (the head) downward.

20. Crimp the tail downward and tuck the edges of the crimp into the pocket shown (tuck in on the far side as well). Mountain-fold the fore- and hind legs downward; repeat behind.

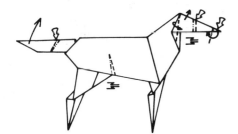

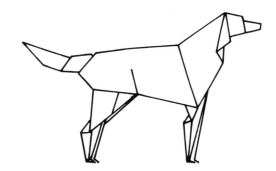

21. Crimp the tail slightly upward and crimp the body just in front of the hind legs to form haunches. The haunch crimps do not go all the way to the top edge, and the body becomes slightly three-dimensional. Fold the flap on the side of the head to the right to make an ear; repeat behind. Shift the head slightly upward. Crimp the head to form a muzzle and reverse-fold the tip.

22. Detail of feet. Crimp all four legs at the tips to form feet. This is best done by reverse-folding the tips backward and then forward.

23. Like this.

24. The finished Irish Setter.

ALLIGATOR

Use a square of paper-backed foil. Begin with the white side up for a colored model. Crease the diagonals.

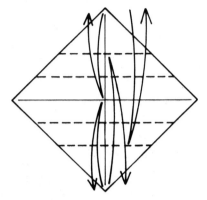

1. Fold the top and bottom corners to the center point, crease, and unfold. Then fold each point so that it touches the opposite crease just made; crease, and unfold.

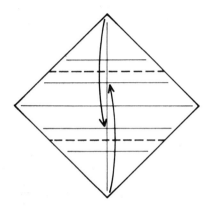

2. Again fold the top and bottom corners so that they touch the creases just made, but this time leave them folded.

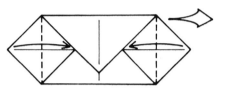

3. Fold the side corners in.

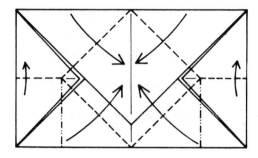

4. Enlarged view. Fold both the right and left sides of the paper into rabbit ears.

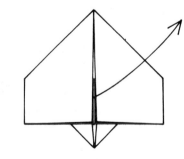

5. Pull the original top corner of the paper out from the interior of the model, forming a flap.

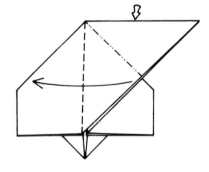

6. Squash-fold the flap.

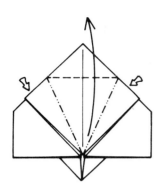

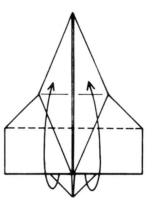

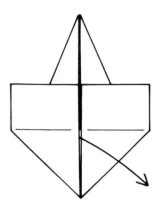

7. Petal-fold the flap.

8. Fold the lower flaps up as far as they will go, folding both layers on each side together as one.

9. Repeat steps 5–8 on the bottom of the model.

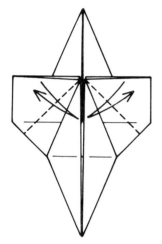

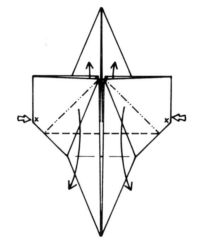

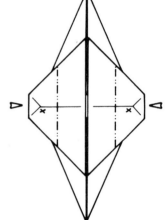

10. Crease the bisectors of the right-angle corners that lie along the center line, creasing through both layers.

11. Squash-fold both sides. The squashed region expands farther than is usual; watch the points marked X.

12. Open-sink the sides inward to the center line.

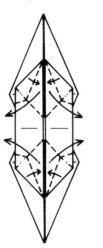

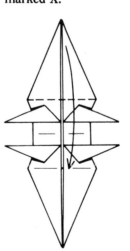

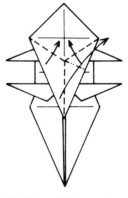

13. Fold a rabbit ear from each of the four flaps that lie along the center line.

14. Fold the top flap down on an existing crease.

15. Fold a rabbit ear from the flap.

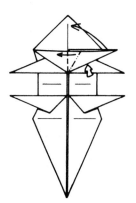

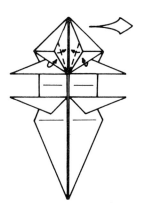

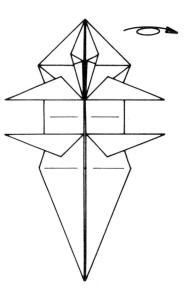

16. Squash-fold the flap upward.

17. Fold the lower sides of the squash-folded flap inward to the center line. Place the upper edges of the two horizontal points over the bottom of the rabbit ear.

18. Enlarged view. Turn the paper over from side to side.

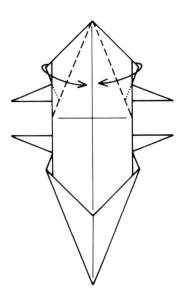

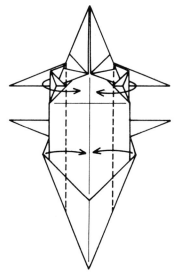

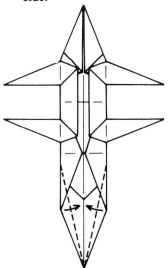

19. Fold the upper edges of the top point to the vertical center line. Small gussets will form at the lower end of each crease.

20. Fold the vertical side edges in toward, but not all the way to, the center line, as far as the bases of the horizontal points (the legs) will allow.

21. Fold the sides of the bottom point inward as shown.

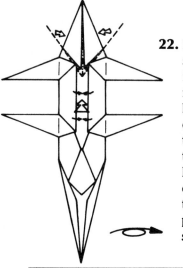

22. Press the far side (the spine) away by pushing inside through the middle of the model and bring the sides toward each other; at the same time, push in the sides of the top near point (the lower jaw) so that the tip of the point moves toward you; turn the paper over from side to side.

23. This shows the same thing from the other side. Make soft mountain folds down the length of the body so that the model is shaped like an inverted U in cross section. Rotate the model a quarter turn clockwise.

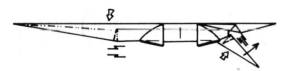

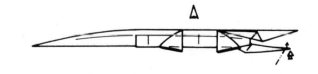

24. Side view of 23 (rotated a quarter turn clockwise). Crimp the right point (the tail) downward. Crimp the lower jaw upward and round it.

25. Reverse-fold the tip of the lower jaw up to form a tooth.

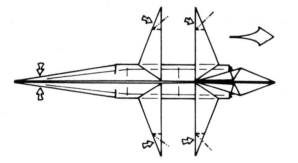

26. Top view of 25. Squash-fold the tips of all four legs forward to form feet. Pinch the tip of the tail.

27. Detail of the right foreleg. Bend it up and curl it down.

28. Repeat on the other three legs.

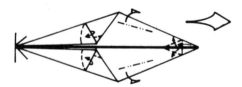

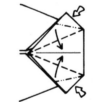

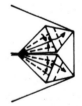

29. Detail of head. Lift up the edges of the eyes to make them round. Curve the sides of the snout away from you, and open out and squash-fold the tip of the nose.

30. Enlarged view of the nose. Squash-fold the flaps on each side.

31. Begin to petal-fold each nostril, but leave the layers standing up in a curved shape at the end of the nose . . .

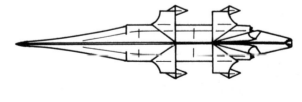

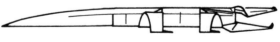

32. . . . like this.

33. Two views of the finished Alligator.

PEGASUS

Use a square, white on both sides. If the paper is colored on one side, begin with the white side up for a white model. Crease the paper in half vertically, horizontally, and diagonally both ways, and crease the angle bisectors at the two side corners.

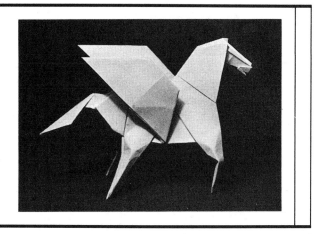

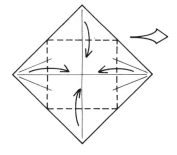

1. Fold each corner to the center point.

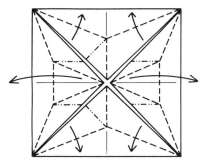

2. Enlarged view. Form rabbit ears from the top and bottom flaps. Fold half of a stretched Bird Base from each side flap.

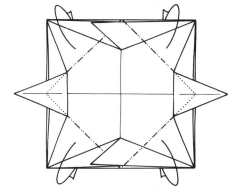

3. Mountain-fold each right-angle corner to the center point behind.

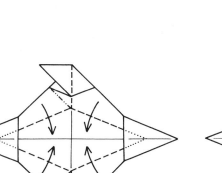

4. Fold both the top and bottom halves of the square shape into rabbit ears. The paper will slide under the triangles on the left and right sides.

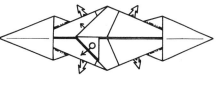

5. Unfold the four flaps on the far side. Pull out the paper from inside each rabbit ear flap.

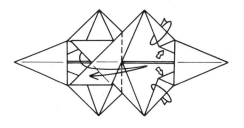

6. Push out the paper on both the upper and lower halves of the right end and wrap it around to the far side. Fold the center flaps to the right and then return them to their former position.

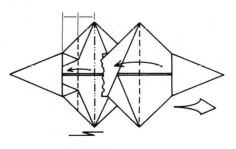

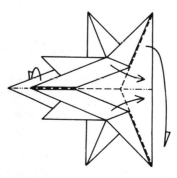

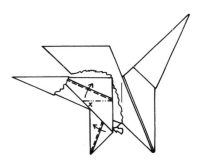

7. Pleat the left end so that the mountain fold that connects the top and bottom corners lies along the base of the left end triangle. Fold the right end to the left along a crease that connects the top and bottom corners.

8. Enlarged view. Fold a rabbit ear from the near flap. At the same time, mountain-fold the top half.

9. Cut-away view, showing the far half from the inside. Swivel by pulling up the upper edge while pushing over the lower layer, flattening it into a collar with its edge aligned with the edge behind it. Watch the X here and in step 10.

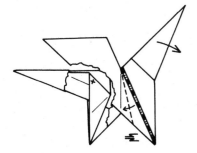

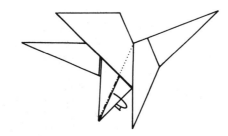

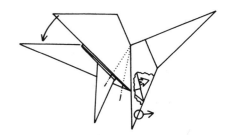

10. Repeat the swivel fold on the near half. Crimp the right end to the left to form the forelegs. Upon completion, the mountain fold will lie along the vertical center crease.

11. Mountain-fold the front of the hind leg to the interior of the leg; repeat behind on the far leg.

12. First pull out the paper from inside the crimp of each foreleg. Then swing the forelegs forward as far as they will easily go. The forelegs and neck swivel upward and the wings downward. The layers inside the base of the wings swivel forward . . .

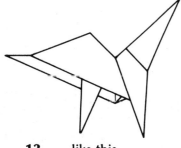

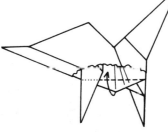

13. . . . like this.

14. Cut-away view showing the far half of the model from the inside. Fold the belly up on the inside of the model.

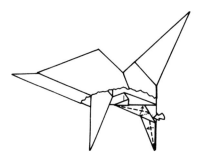

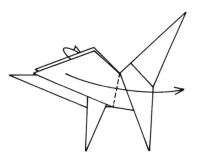

15. Cut-away view showing the far half of the model from the inside. Swivel the layers, forming a collar on the foreleg with its edge aligned with the edges behind it.

16. Repeat steps 14 and 15 on the other foreleg.

17. Swing the wings to the front.

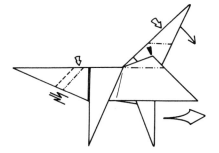

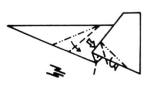

18. Closed-sink the top corner of each wing so that the resulting edges are parallel to the bottom edges of the wing. Reverse-fold the top point of the neck downward to form a head. Crimp the hindquarters, keeping the top edge horizontal.

19. Enlarged view. Crimp the tail. Swivel the rear corner of the rump inside; repeat behind.

20. Swivel the paper at the base of the tail, forming a collar inside with its edge flush with the line of the tail; repeat behind.

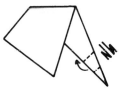

21. Mountain-fold the point at the base of the tail inside the model; repeat behind . . .

22. . . . like this.

23. Pleat the nose with outside reverse folds.

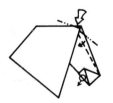

24. Form ears by swiveling each top front corner of the head so that the edges at the front of the ears are aligned. Open the mouth slightly . . .

25. . . . like this.

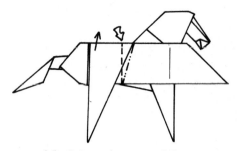

26. Crimp the rear of the body upward. The mountain fold lies on the crease at the base of the wing and the valley fold is perpendicular to the edge of the back.

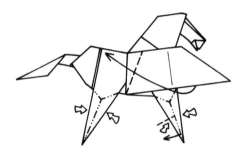

27. Pinch the sides of the legs to narrow them and bend the forelegs backward at the knees. Fold the wings upward and slightly backward.

28. The finished Pegasus.

CAMEL

Use a square the same color on both sides. If the paper is colored on one side only, begin with the white side up for a colored model.

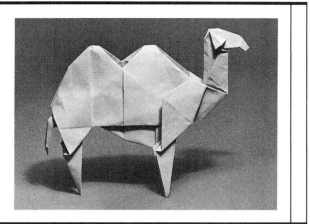

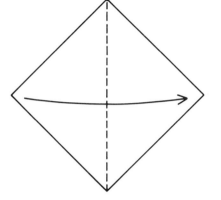

1. Fold the paper in half vertically along the diagonal.

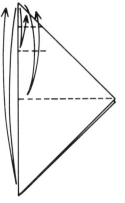

2. Bring the bottom point up to the top, crease, and unfold. Then fold the top point down to that crease, make a small pinch, and unfold. Finally, fold the top point down to the last crease, pinch, and unfold.

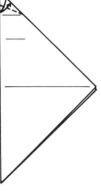

3. Fold the right edge of the top corner down to the last crease, pinch, and unfold.

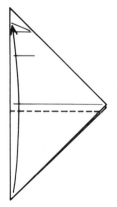

4. Fold the bottom up to the point at which the last crease meets the folded edge.

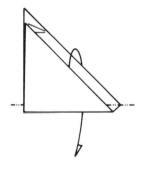

5. Mountain-fold the far point on an existing crease.

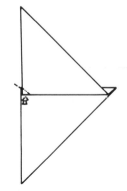

6. Reverse-fold the left near corner of the pleat.

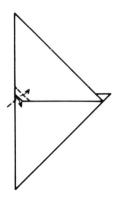

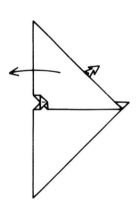

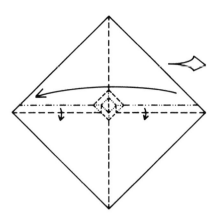

7. Spread the layers shown and flatten out the reverse-fold made in step 6.

8. Open the paper out completely.

9. Refold on the existing creases as shown.

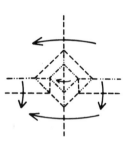

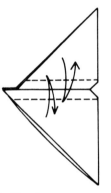

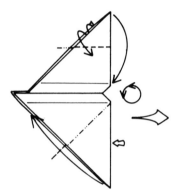

10. This is a close-up of the fold lines in the center of the paper.

11. The layers are now symmetrical. Crease as shown. Note that the valley folds lie slightly above and below the corners on the right side.

12. Outside-reverse-fold the top point down to the intersection of the edge with the upper crease. Inside-reverse-fold the bottom point so that its left edge is aligned with the lower crease. Rotate the model a quarter turn counterclockwise.

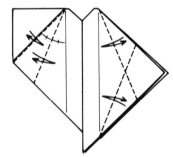

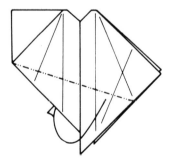

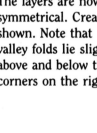

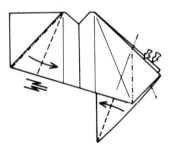

13. Enlarged view. Crease along the raw edge of the triangular corner at the left. Bring the edge down to the vertical crease, crease, and unfold. Crease· a double layer of paper on the right; repeat behind.

14. Mountain-fold the pleated layer as shown; repeat behind.

15. Crimp the left side of the model. Inside-reverse-fold the right side; repeat behind.

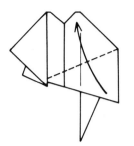

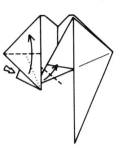

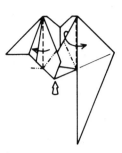

16. Fold the lower right flap as far up as possible; repeat behind.

17. Fold upward the point at the bottom left and squash-fold the layers behind it; repeat behind.

18. Squash-fold the indicated point while swiveling each side outward along a vertical valley fold; repeat behind.

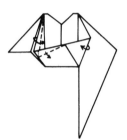

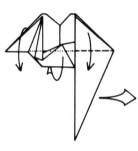

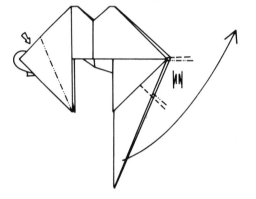

19. Swivel the layers on the left. Tuck the layers on the right under the raw edge of paper. Repeat behind.

20. Swing both points down and swing the layers at the bottom middle upward inside the model; repeat behind.

21. Enlarged view. Reverse-fold the left corner. Crimp upward the long lower point at the right.

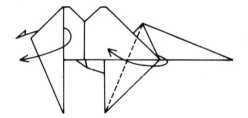

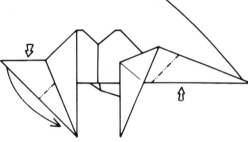

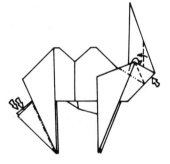

22. Unwrap the layer of paper on the left side. Fold the flap shown at the right; repeat behind.

23. Reverse-fold the corner at the left down to the bottom points. Reverse-fold the long point at the right (the neck and head).

24. Reverse-fold both corners at the lower left. Swivel the front of the neck in; repeat behind.

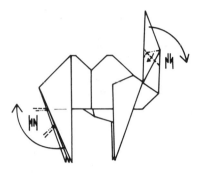

25. Crimp upward the middle point at the left (the tail). Crimp the top of the neck down to form a head, pushing in the top corner of the crimp (see steps 26–28).

26. This shows one way to accomplish the head crimp. First, reverse-fold the top point.

27. Then make an outside-reverse-fold slightly offset from the left corner of the inside reverse fold.

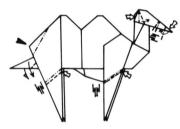

28. Pull the excess paper out from under the cheek on each side; pull the head down slightly and pinch to flatten it.

29. Closed-sink the rear corner of the rump. Outside-reverse-fold the tail. Crimp the legs and squash-fold the ear; repeat behind. Crimp the muzzle and reverse-fold the tip of it inside.

30. Closed-sink the tail to narrow it.

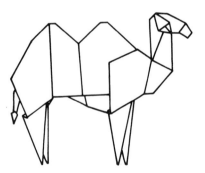

31. Enlarged view of tail. Crimp the tip upward.

32. Pull the layers out from the inside of the tip of the tail to form a tuft.

33. The finished Camel.

Mouse

Use a square the same color on both sides. If the square is colored on one side only, begin with the white side up for a colored model. Crease the vertical diagonal.

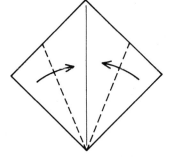

1. Fold the lower edges into the center line.

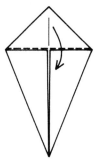

2. Fold the triangular top down over the two side flaps.

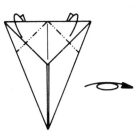

3. Mountain-fold the top edge on each side to the center line. Turn the model over from side to side.

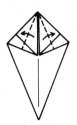

4. Fold the edges that lie along the center line to the outer edges.

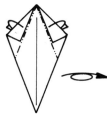

5. Mountain-fold the pleated layers. Turn the model over from side to side.

6. Unfold the paper to step 1.

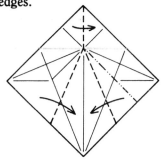

7. Fold a rabbit ear on existing creases.

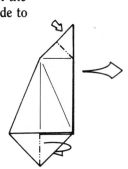

8. Reverse-fold the top corner of the rabbit ear. Mountain-fold the right layer behind the rabbit ear to the left.

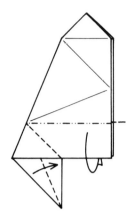

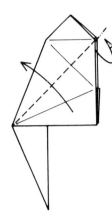

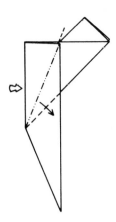

9. Enlarged view. Swivel the near layer shown to the inside; repeat behind. The mountain fold is horizontal.

10. Fold the flap shown to the left; repeat behind.

11. Squash-fold the upper left corner; repeat behind.

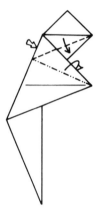

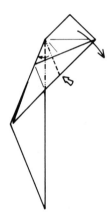

12. Swivel the near upper layers; repeat behind.

13. Fold a rabbit ear; repeat behind.

14. Crimp in front and back, pushing in the lower edges; the top of the model pivots downward.

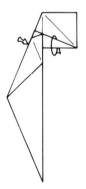

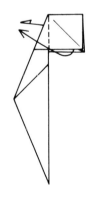

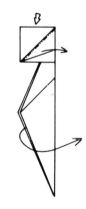

15. Wrap around to the inside the layers shown; repeat behind.

16. Outside-reverse-fold the top of the model.

17. Squash-fold the top left corner and swing the near side of the model to the right.

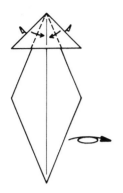 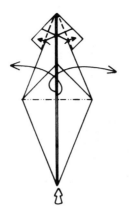 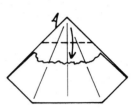

18. Fold the upper edges in to the center and let the edges at the center on the far side swing outward. Turn the model over from side to side.

19. Pull the edges at the center out to the sides and bring the bottom point up to the top point.

20. Fold the top of the far layer downward; the points folded to the center in step 18 swing upward.

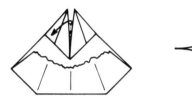  

21. Pull the inner layer of paper out from between the top points to form a flap.

22. Only the top of the model is shown in steps 22–27 (and the view is enlarged). Squash-fold the flap.

23. Petal-fold.

  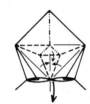

24. Unwrap the single layer of paper from around the petal fold.

25. Perform a *closed wrap* on each side of the petal fold, bringing two layers from behind to the front (see Procedures, page 24).

26. By partially opening out the paper, you can accomplish step 25 with this crease pattern. (View is reduced 50%.)

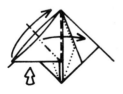 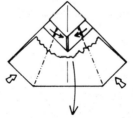

27. Squash-fold the flap.

28. Full view of model. Swing down the near layer of paper (shown partially cut away) and push in the sides (this undoes step 19).

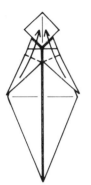
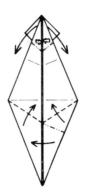
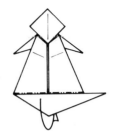

29. Fold the flap on each side as far up as possible.

30. Reverse-fold the two points at the top. Fold a rabbit ear from the bottom of the model.

31. Mountain-fold the rabbit ear.

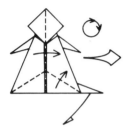
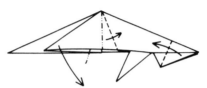
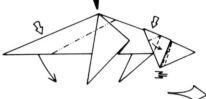

32. Fold the model in half from left to right, incorporating the reverse fold at the bottom, which swings the far point down. Rotate the model a quarter turn clockwise.

33. Enlarged view. Swivel the large flap in the middle downward with a pleat on the near layer. This forms a hind leg. Fold one point at the right up and to the left (an ear). Repeat behind.

34. Closed-sink the top corner, reversing the long edge at the upper left (the tail). Squash-fold the ear; repeat behind. Crimp the head.

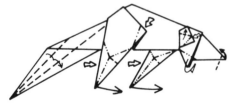

35. Fold the tail over and over in thirds. Fold a *double rabbit ear* from the hind leg (see Procedures, page 23). Reverse-fold the front corner of the haunch. Fold a double rabbit ear from the foreleg. Swivel the ear up. Mountain-fold to the inside the point at the bottom of the head. Repeat behind. Reverse-fold the tip of the nose.

36. Crimp the base of the tail.

37. The finished Mouse.

WOOLLY MAMMOTH

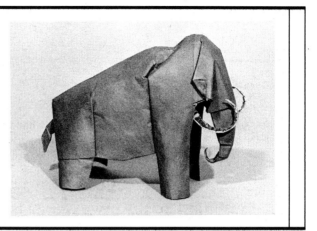

Use a square of paper-backed foil. Begin with the white side up. Crease the paper in half horizontally.

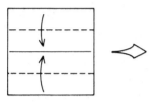

1. Fold the top and bottom edges to the horizontal center crease.

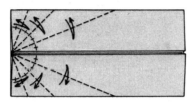

2. Enlarged view. Divide the angle of each corner at center left into fourths (this can be done by dividing each into halves, and then dividing each of those into halves). Crease through both the near and far layers.

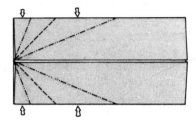

3. Reverse-fold the upper and lower left corners in and out, using the creases just made.

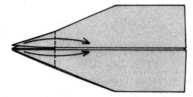

4. Fold the two narrow left points as far to the right as they will go.

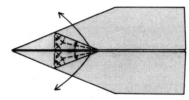

5. Fold a rabbit ear from each of the narrow points.

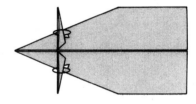

6. Wrap a single layer of paper from the near to the far side of each rabbit ear, changing its color.

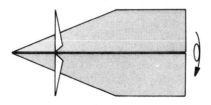

7. Turn the paper over from top to bottom.

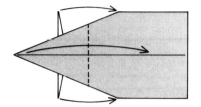 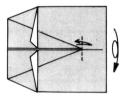 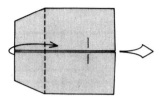

8. Fold the left side of the model over to the right, so that the tips of the two narrow white points touch the upper and lower corners of the colored part of the model. Be sure the right edges of the points are perpendicular to the center line.

9. Make a short valley fold through the far flap where the near point ends. Turn the paper over from top to bottom.

10. Fold the left portion of the model over toward the right, forming a crease that connects the upper and lower corners; allow the hidden point behind to swing out to the left.

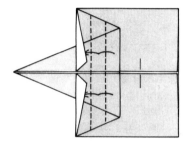 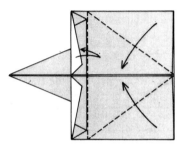 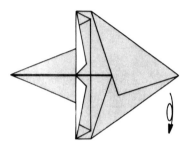

11. Enlarged view. Fold the layers at the middle of the model over and over in thirds to the left and tuck them under the two narrow white points.

12. Crease the left portion of the model along a vertical valley fold aligned with the thick vertical folded edge. Fold in the upper and lower right corners, forming creases that connect the midpoint of the right side with the ends of the vertical crease. The corners will overlap . . .

13. . . . like this. Turn the paper over from top to bottom.

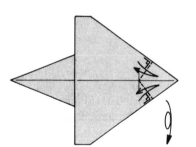 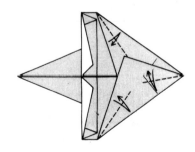 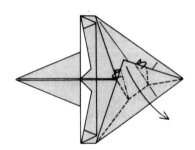

14. Crease two valley folds that extend to the edges from the intersection of the horizontal center crease and the crease made in step 9; the valley folds are at right angles to the edges. Turn the paper over from top to bottom.

15. Crease the angle bisectors of the two overlapping flaps.

16. On the lower flap, fold the flap down to the right and swivel each of the edges, using as a guide the creases of step 15 and the intersection of the creases made in steps 14 and 15; repeat on the upper flap.

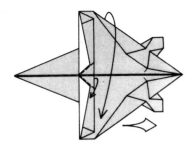

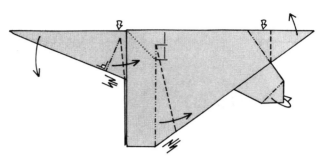

17. Fold the model in half, top to bottom, incorporating the small reverse fold in the thick layers between the two white points.

18. Enlarged view. Crimp the left point (the head) downward. Crimp the body just behind the thick layers; this crimp does not go all the way to the top of the model, and the body therefore becomes three-dimensional. Crimp the tail with two reverse folds. Mountain-fold the bottom of the hind leg; repeat behind.

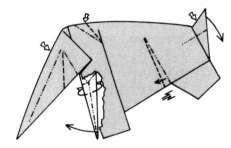

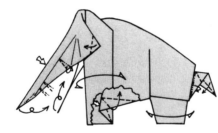

19. Crimp the head again to define the trunk. Fold a rabbit ear from each white point and swing it forward to make a tusk. Crimp the body just in front of the hind legs; the crimp does not run all the way to the top of the model. Press in the back of the head at the top of the forelegs. Reverse-fold the tail downward.

20. Crimp the trunk downward at three places and curl the tip inward. Curl the tusks upward. Fold the ear forward; repeat behind. The cut-away view shows the inside of the far foreleg. Swivel it upward to lock the crimp and shape the belly; repeat on the near leg. Swivel the tail to narrow it; repeat behind. Curve the legs to round and narrow them.

21. Detail of tail. Squash-fold the tail downward on each side, pushing up the middle layers.

22. The finished Woolly Mammoth.

DOG IN A DOGHOUSE

Use a square of paper-backed foil. Begin with the white side up. Crease the paper in half horizontally.

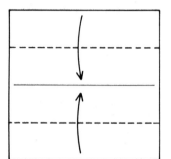

1. Fold the top and bottom edges to the horizontal center crease.

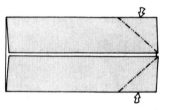

2. Reverse-fold the upper and lower right corners.

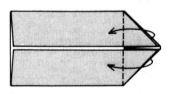

3. Fold the two near right points to the left as far as possible.

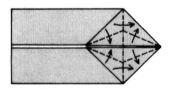

4. Fold each point back to the right, incorporating the reverse fold shown into the near layer.

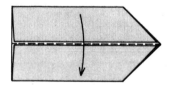

5. Fold the model in half lengthwise, from top to bottom.

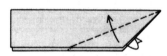

6. Fold up the near right edge so that it lies along the top edge; repeat behind.

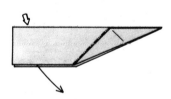

7. Reverse-fold the left end downward; the crease aligns with the edges of the flaps folded up in step 6.

8. Pull a single layer of paper out from the inside and wrap it upward in the front; repeat behind.

9. Fold one flap from the left over to the right.

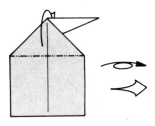

10. Mountain-fold to the rear the top triangular portion of the model, along with the three white points. Turn the model over from side to side.

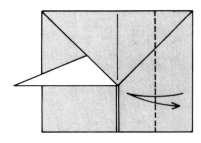

11. Enlarged view. Fold the right edge in to the vertical center line, crease, and unfold.

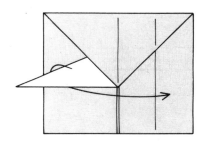

12. Swing the three white points to the right.

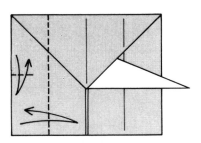

13. Fold the left edge in to the center line, crease, and unfold. Then fold the top edge down to the bottom edge, make a small crease at the left edge only, and unfold.

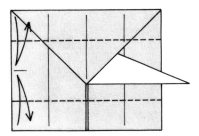

14. Fold the top and bottom edges to the short crease just made and make a sharp crease all the way across the model, being careful not to let the layers slip. Unfold.

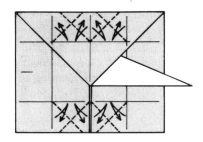

15. Crease the four pairs of angle bisectors shown.

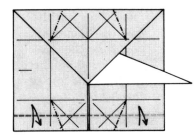

16. Crease each of the two pairs of angle bisectors shown at the top and bottom as mountain folds (turn the paper over and make valley folds). Fold the bottom edge up to the horizontal crease and unfold.

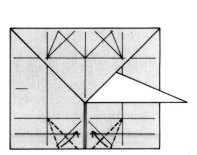

17. Pleat the bottom of the model using the existing creases. The model will no longer lie flat.

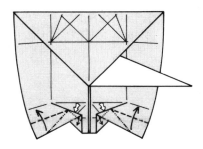

18. Swivel the bottom edge upward on each side.

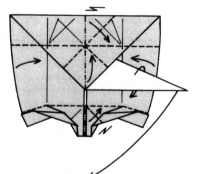

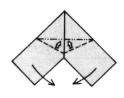

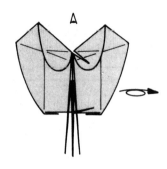

19. Fold the top edge down and the bottom edges up while moving the sides inward; make two pleats, one at the top and one at the bottom, to take in the excess paper. Lift the base of the three white points toward you and swing the points down through the opening at the bottom. The model remains three-dimensional.

20. Turn the paper over from side to side.

21. View from step 20. Pleat the back on existing creases where shown and bring the sides together . . .

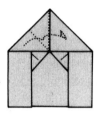

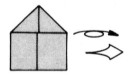

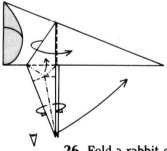

22. . . . like this; the model is fully three-dimensional. Turn the model over from side to side.

23. Enlarged view; the three white points are not shown, but if they were, they would be pointing directly at you through the opening in the middle of the model. Fold the hidden flap indicated by X-ray lines over and over on the inside to lock the sides together.

24. Perspective view of the model thus far. The colored region is the doghouse; the three white points will become the head and forelegs of the dog.

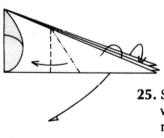

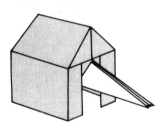

25. Side view of the three white points. Pleat the near and far points downward. To make steps 25–33 easier, undo the lock made in step 23 and open the house somewhat; close the house when finished.

26. Fold a rabbit ear from the downward-pointing flap, raising it up. Swing the entire flap to the right; repeat behind.

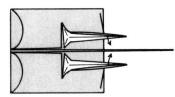

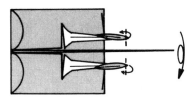

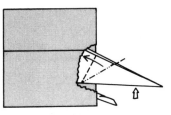

27. Bottom view of the doghouse. Spread the layers at the tip of each leg to form paws.

28. Fold the tip of each paw inward to blunt it. Turn the model over from top to bottom so that it is upright.

29. Side view. Squash-fold the remaining (middle) white point upward. Note that the squash fold extends left into the doghouse.

30. Details of the dog's head. Squash-fold the flap downward, opening it out as much as possible.

31. Mountain-fold the right side behind.

32. Fold the upper left edge down to form an ear; repeat behind. Crimp the head with two reverse folds to form a muzzle; you will have to lift up the head to do this. Outside-reverse-fold the tip of the nose.

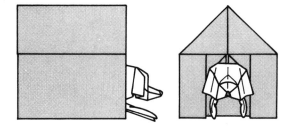

33. Pull the head forward while pushing in the top of the head and muzzle to flatten them and make them three-dimensional.

34. Two views of the finished Dog in a Doghouse.

BEAR

Use a rectangle of proportions 3:5, the same color on both sides. If the paper is colored on one side only, begin with the white side up for a predominantly colored model. Make a vertical crease ⅖ of the way from the left to the right side, and divide the short side into sixths with horizontal creases.

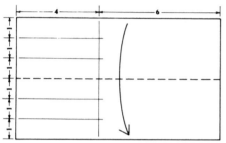

1. Fold the paper in half lengthwise, from top to bottom.

2. Crease the bisector of the angle formed by the vertical crease and the bottom horizontal edge; crease through both layers of paper.

3. Fold the left side downward and to the right along a crease that connects the two intersections shown. The crease goes no farther than is explicitly shown, so the paper will not lie completely flat.

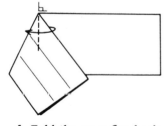

4. Fold the near flap back to the left along a vertical crease (the fold aligns with an existing crease on the far flap); note the right-angle indicator.

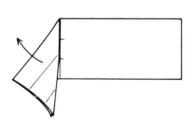

5. Unfold to step 2.

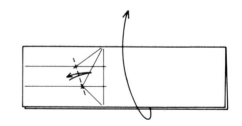

6. With another crease through both layers, connect the two crease intersections shown; then open the paper completely.

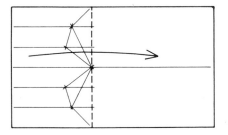

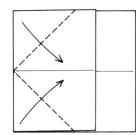

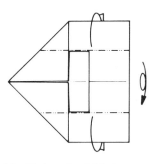

7. Fold the left side over to the right on the existing vertical crease.

8. Fold the upper and lower halves of the left edge so that they lie along the horizontal crease.

9. Turn the paper over from top to bottom.

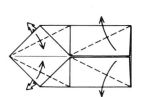

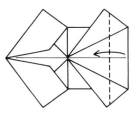

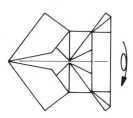

10. Fold the top and bottom edges to the horizontal center crease line and unfold. Turn the paper over from top to bottom.

11. On existing creases, mountain-fold to the inside the layers that are between the near and far surfaces.

12. Mountain-fold the top and bottom edges to the center line. Turn the paper over from top to bottom.

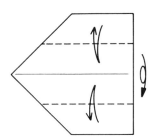

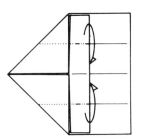

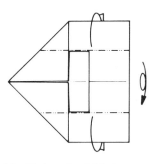

13. Fold the upper and lower left corners inward, allowing the loose layers of paper behind to swing outward. On the right side of the model, fold the upper and lower corners at the center line outward.

14. Fold the right edge over to the left, so that the upper and lower right corners touch the raw edges of the paper.

15. Turn the paper over from top to bottom.

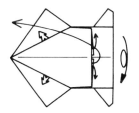

16. Pull the original left corners of the rectangle out and to the left, releasing (as shown) the trapped layers of paper from the pockets. Turn the paper over from top to bottom; the paper will not lie flat.

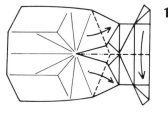

17. Fold the right side of the model partially in half, and incorporate the reverse fold creases in the central part of the model, which forms a pyramid pointing toward you.

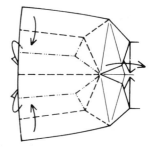

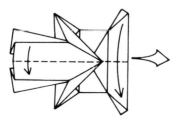

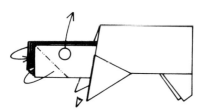

18. Make these creases, which were formed in steps 1–6, into the folds shown.

19. Fold the model in half lengthwise, from top to bottom; it will lie flat when closed.

20. Enlarged view. Mountain-fold the near left corner and valley-fold the far left corner inside. To lift the pleated portion of the model upward, allow the sides of the model to spread, and open the pleated portion symmetrically from the bottom.

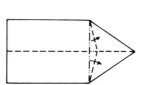

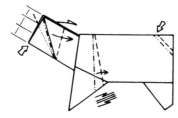

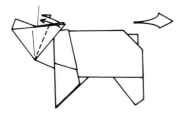

21. View of the underside of the pleated portion of the model. Incorporate this crimp on the single near layer and close the model, pressing the sides together, with the pleated portion raised as far as it will go.

22. Squash-fold the near left corner; repeat behind. Crimp the sides of the body, leaving the inner structure uncrimped. Form a tail with two reverse folds.

23. Fold the ears forward on each side to the point shown.

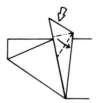

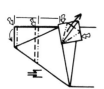

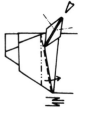

24. Enlarged view of the head. Squash-fold the ear; repeat behind.

25. Crimp the head to form a muzzle and reverse-fold the front edge of the nose. Petal-fold the ear; repeat behind.

26. Crimp the head downward. Sink the tip of the ear; repeat behind.

27. Cut-away view, showing the far ear. Fold down the small point on the inner side of the far ear; repeat on the near ear (not shown).

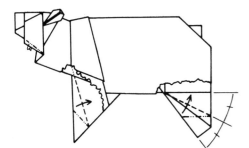 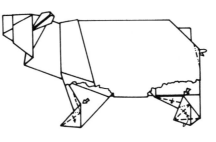 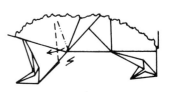

28. Mountain-fold the lower edge of the head to the inside; repeat behind. Pleat the far fore- and hind leg (shown in cut-away view) with a swivel; repeat on the near legs.

29. Swivel the edges of the far fore- and hind legs, and fold the bottom of the far hind leg upward; repeat on the near legs.

30. Cut-away view of the far legs and inner structure. Crimp the inner structure just to the rear of the foreleg so that it matches the line of the leg made by the crimp in step 22; repeat on the near side. The layers inside may not lie completely flat after this crimp, but that is not important.

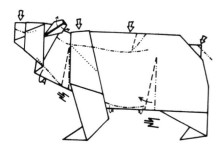  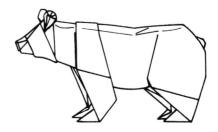

31. Push down on the nose and back to make the model three-dimensional. Reverse-fold the tip of the tail. Crimp the body slightly in front of the hind legs. Mountain-fold the belly; repeat behind. Crimp the neck downward. Mountain-fold the bottom of the neck; repeat behind. Spread open and round out the ears.

32. Detail of the near hind leg crimp. Reverse-fold the corner shown; repeat behind.

33. The finished Bear.

GOLDEN EAGLE

Use a square the same color on both sides. If the paper is colored on one side only, begin with the white side up for a predominantly colored model. Crease the square in half both vertically and horizontally.

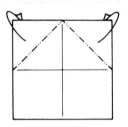

1. Mountain-fold the two upper corners behind to the center point.

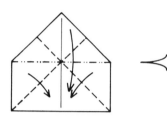

2. Fold as shown to form a combination of a Preliminary Fold and a *Waterbomb Base* (see Procedures, page 16).

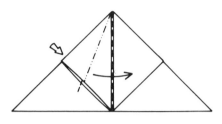

3. Enlarged view. Squash-fold the left flap.

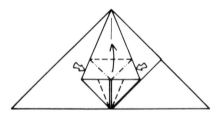

4. Petal-fold the squashed flap.

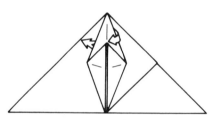

5. Unwrap the layer of paper from around the petal fold and reposition as shown in the next drawing.

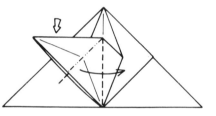

6. Squash-fold the new flap.

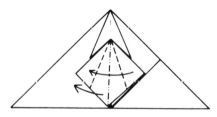

7. Swing the right side of the flap to the left, pulling out the middle of the paper so that it aligns with the upper edges.

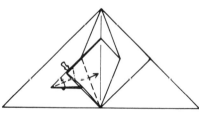

8. Simultaneously make the two valley folds, squash-folding the corner of the near flap to allow completion.

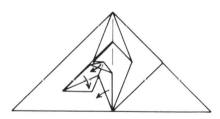

9. Unfold.

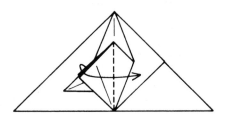

10. Swing the three aligned layers to the right.

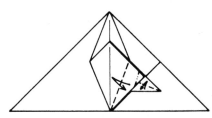

11. Repeat steps 8 and 9 on this side.

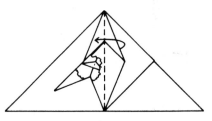

12. Unfold the paper to step 7.

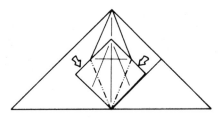

13. Reverse-fold the corners as shown.

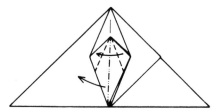

14. Swing the right side of the near flap to the left, pulling up the middle of the paper so that it aligns with the upper edges. The interior layers assume the configuration of the folds made in steps 8 and 9.

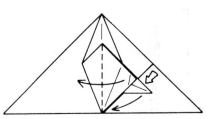

15. Fold the near right flap to the left.

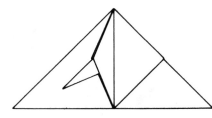

16. Repeat steps 3–15 on the right side.

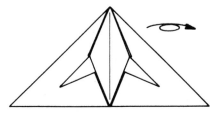

17. Turn the paper over from side to side.

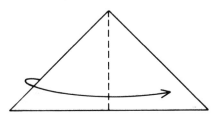

18. Swing the large left flap to the right.

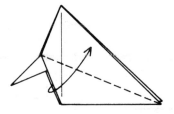

19. Fold the near layer up.

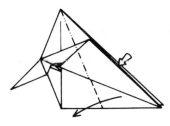

20. Reverse-fold the flap shown; note the location of the mountain-fold line and the valley-fold line.

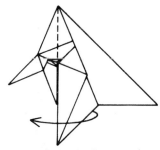

21. Fold both flaps to the left.

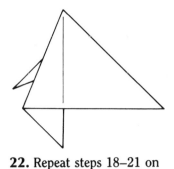

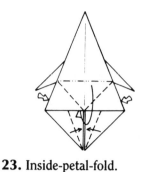

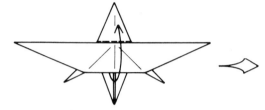

22. Repeat steps 18–21 on the right.

23. Inside-petal-fold.

24. Reverse-fold the two bottom flaps out as far as possible.

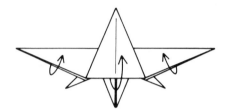

25. Wrap one layer from the inside to the outside.

26. Lift up the wide flap.

27. Enlarged view of the bottom point. Push the tip of the bottom point up on the near side; simultaneously make a very narrow squash fold of the layers on each side of the center line.

28. Pull the raw edges of the paper out to the sides.

29. Wrap the bottom layer around to the far side.

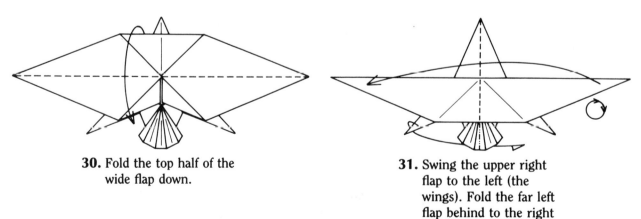

30. Fold the top half of the wide flap down.

31. Swing the upper right flap to the left (the wings). Fold the far left flap behind to the right (the feet). Rotate the model a quarter turn clockwise.

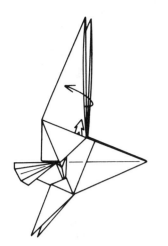

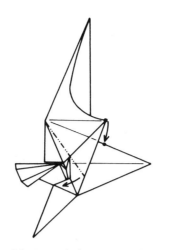

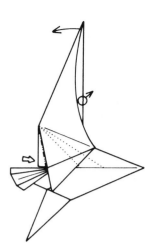

32. Lift the single rear layer of the wing and pull the loose paper out of the model.

33. Swivel the excess paper so that the indicated corner lies on the edge of the model; repeat behind. The wings still do not lie flat.

34. Roll the layers at the back of the wings (just above the tail) inward; at the same time, pull the wing tips to the left, allowing the interior layers of each wing to swivel to the right at the bottom. The old and new interior creases are indicated by the X-ray lines. The model will now lie flat.

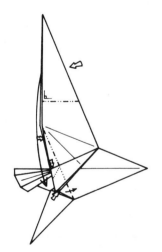

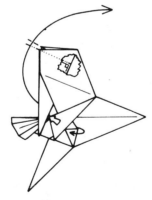

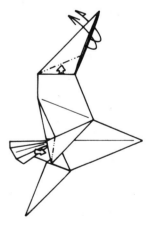

35. Reverse-fold the tip of each wing so that the left edges are aligned and the tip touches the bottom edge of the body below the tail. Make the interlinked reverse folds shown at the base of the wing. To make the folds continuous, the middle layer is pushed down inside the top left corner of the triangular layer.

36. Reverse-fold the tip of each wing upward as shown. At the base of each wing, use a closed wrap to turn the indicated corner inside out, so that it lies between the two layers originally behind it.

37. Pull out the trapped paper from the near and far layers of the wing; repeat behind on the other wing. Reverse-fold the corner at the base of each wing.

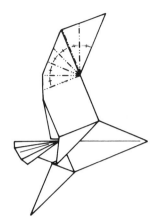

38. Crease only the near layers of the wing with mountain folds. Crease both layers of the protruding tip together as one.

39. The mountain folds stay where they are; add a valley fold to each one to form pleats. When all the pleats are made, all of the wing tip paper will be on the near side.

40. Crease this part of the wing back and forth.

41. Unfold the indicated pleats.

42. Fold the indicated part behind and restore the pleats. Closed-sink the corner formed by the trailing edge of the wing.

43. Reverse-fold the far corner of each pleat, right, left, right, so that the near corner of each one comes to a point.

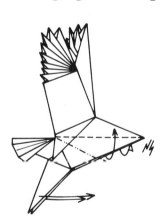

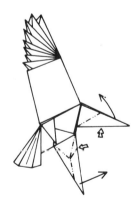

44. Closed-sink the edge shown. Repeat steps 38–44 on the other wing.

45. Spread the layers at the bottom evenly to the near and far sides and crimp upward; the legs and tail move forward.

46. Reverse-fold the head. Fold a double rabbit ear from each leg. Notice that the mountain fold does not go to the tip.

47. Enlarged view of head. Crimp the head down.

48. Crimp the beak and reverse-fold its tip down.

49. Enlarged view of leg. Reverse-fold the tip of the foot.

50. Narrow each leg with mountain folds to the inside. Dent the front edge of each foot to make three talons out of the top and two bottom corners.

51. Spread the wings. Pinch the body at the base of the tail to make it three-dimensional. Fluff the layers of paper above the legs. Reverse-fold forward the rear talon on each foot.

52. The finished Golden Eagle.

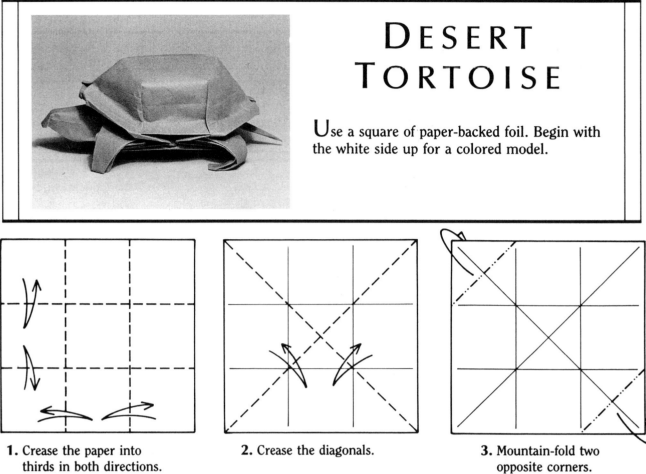

DESERT TORTOISE

Use a square of paper-backed foil. Begin with the white side up for a colored model.

1. Crease the paper into thirds in both directions.

2. Crease the diagonals.

3. Mountain-fold two opposite corners.

4. Fold two interlocking rabbit ears; all folds occur on existing creases. Turn the paper over.

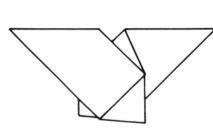

5. Flatten the model.

6. Squash-fold the upper left flap; repeat behind with the opposite flap.

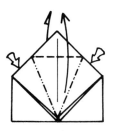

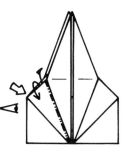

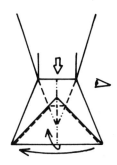

7. Petal-fold the squashed flap; repeat behind.

8. Reverse-fold the upper left corner of the broadest part of the model. Open out the paper to do this.

9. Side view. Push down where shown and add the creases shown. Close the model again.

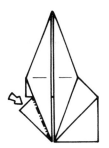

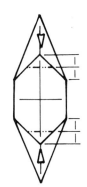

10. Reverse-fold the protruding lower corner on the left side. Repeat steps 8–10 on the right.

11. Fold the near flap down as far as possible.

12. Open-sink the corners shown.

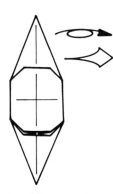

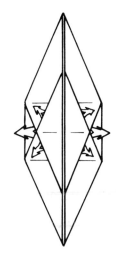

13. Turn the paper over from side to side.

14. Enlarged view. Fold the near flap up on both the left and right.

15. Grasping the left and right corners that are hidden in the layers along the sides, pull the trapped layers of paper out from each side.

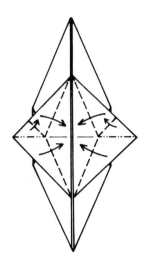

16. On each side fold a rabbit ear with the flap inside (note that this is not the usual rabbit ear made from this shape).

17. Fold up the near flap on each side.

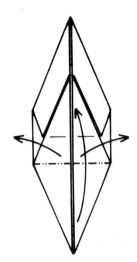

18. Lift up the bottom point and spread the raw edges (this is the inverse of a petal fold).

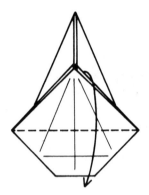

19. Fold all three points downward.

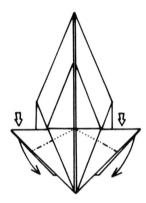

20. Reverse-fold the two points shown so that their outermost edges are vertical.

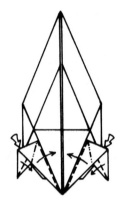

21. Swivel a double layer of paper on the left and right.

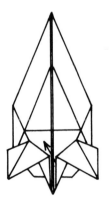

22. Pull out the hidden point from the right and stretch it as far as is easily possible.

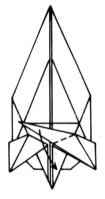

23. Fold the point back down again.

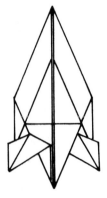

24. . . . like this. Repeat steps 22 and 23 on the left.

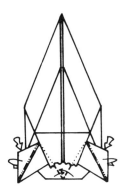

25. The head is shown cut away (for clarity only). Swivel as shown.

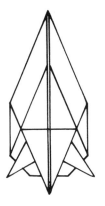

26. Repeat steps 17–25 on the top of the model.

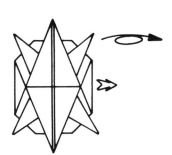

27. Unfold the model to step 17 and turn it over.

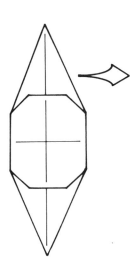

28. It looks like this.

32. Top view. Mountain-fold the tiny corners at the base of the pleats. Turn the model over from side to side and refold the legs, returning them to the configuration of step 27. (The reason for unfolding it is that the shell must be shaped from the inside; but with the leg folds in place, the inside is inaccessible. For this reason, be careful not to dent the shell for the rest of the folding sequence because you won't be able to get to the inside to repair it.)

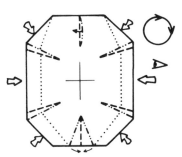

29. Only the shell is shown here. Reach inside and push the center of the shell upward. At the same time, push in the sides all around and form pleats where shown. As the sides are pushed in, the paper beneath the outer edges slides upward. New outer edges are formed by this paper along the X-ray lines. As the shell assumes a dome shape, the outer edges in drawing 29 become the crease marks seen on the lower part of the shell in subsequent drawings. Rotate the model a quarter turn clockwise.

30. Side view. Note the position of the pleats and note that they extend past the former outer edges (crease marks) to the new ones, which were the X-ray lines in drawing 29. Closed-sink the top left corner to round the shell. Repeat on the far side. Push down at the base of the shell all around to form a rim. Shape the right side so that the rim curves upward; this will be the side closest to the head . . .

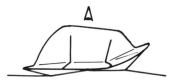

31. . . . like this.

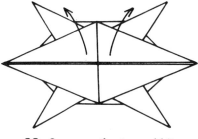

33. Open up the top rabbit ear.

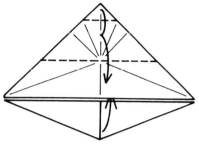

34. Tuck the bottom rabbit ear behind the top flap. Fold the top flap over and over downward. (The legs are not shown here.)

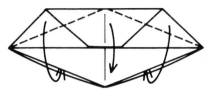

35. Wrap the top flap over the bottom one and tuck the corners into the pockets shown at the bottom edge.

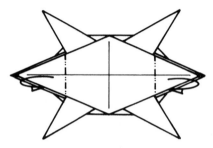

36. Mountain-fold the left and right points of the near surface into the model. This finishes locking the lower shell.

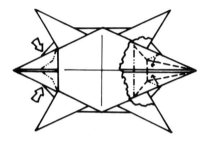

37. Pinch and make three-dimensional the point on the left, which should be the head. Pleat and narrow the tail; the folds all take place hidden by the lower shell.

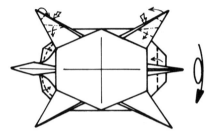

38. Fold the rim over in front and back to complete locking and to shape the shell. Stretch the legs into shape (see final diagrams for an example, but you can shape them several ways). Turn the model over from top to bottom.

39. Squash-fold the nose.

40. Mountain-fold the tip to the inside of the head.

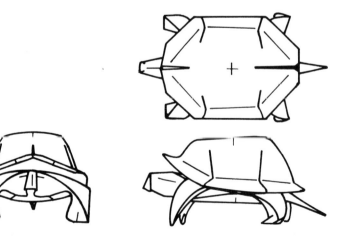

41. Three views of the finished Desert Tortoise.

RABBIT

Use a square of paper-backed foil. Begin with the white side up for a predominantly colored model.

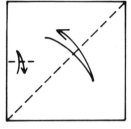

1. Crease the diagonal from the bottom left corner to the top right corner, and make a pinch mark dividing the left side in half.

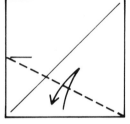

2. Make a crease from the left edge at the pinch mark to the bottom right corner.

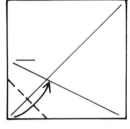

3. Fold the bottom left corner in to touch the intersection of the crease just made and the diagonal of the square.

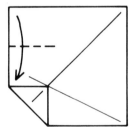

4. Fold the top edge down so that it lies along the folded-in corner and pinch a crease for about a third of the way across the square.

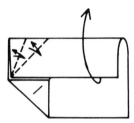

5. Fold and unfold as shown, creasing both layers, and then open the top of the paper.

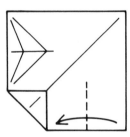

6. Repeat steps 4 and 5 on the adjacent part of the square.

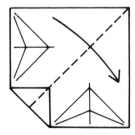

7. Fold the paper in half diagonally.

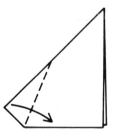

8. Fold the bottom left over so that it aligns with the bottom edges.

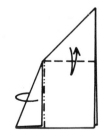

9. Fold the left side behind along the edge of the near layers. Fold the top down so that the right edges are aligned, and raise it up again.

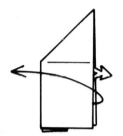

10. Open the paper, returning it to the configuration of step 7.

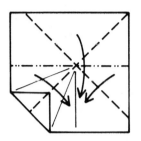

11. Fold the square as if you were making an off-center Waterbomb Base, using the existing creases as a guide.

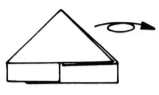

12. Turn the paper over from side to side.

13. Squash-fold the indicated flap.

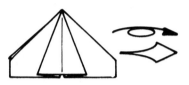

14. Turn the paper over from side to side.

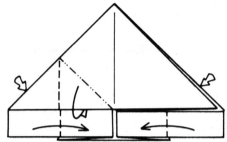

15. Enlarged view. Fold the left side in while swiveling the extra paper of the near layer inside; repeat on the right.

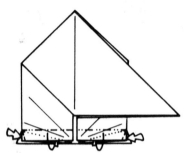

16. Reverse-fold the bottom corners as shown. Note that the horizontal mountain folds meet the vertical outer edges where the slanted layers behind meet them.

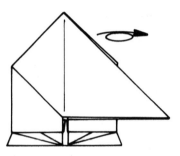

17. Turn the model over from side to side.

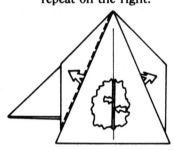

18. Pull out the inside layers so that the inner folded edges are inverted and aligned with the model's outer edges.

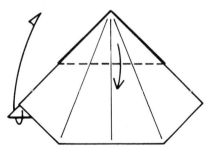

19. Fold the top of the model down allowing the large flap behind to swing upward.

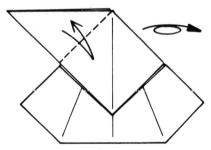

20. Fold the upper left corner to the lower central corner and unfold. Turn the model over from side to side.

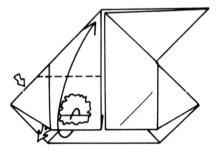

21. Open the mountain fold of step 15 and bring the corner of the original square up to the top of the model and crease. The paper will not lie flat.

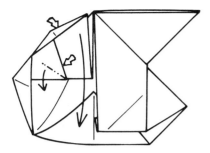 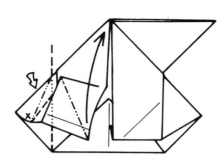 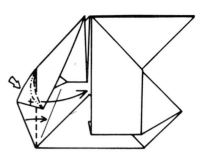

22. Squash the layers shown inside the pocket and flatten out the top of the flap along an existing crease.

23. Mountain-fold in half the loose point and bring it to the top again. At the same time push in the side along a vertical valley fold and start forming the mountain and valley pleats along the edge. Watch the position of X in the next two drawings.

24. Partway done. Continue to flatten the model entirely, aligning the top left edges and the vertical center edges.

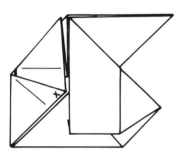 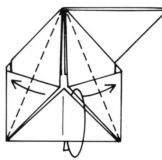 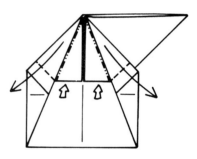

25. Repeat steps 21–24 on the right.

26. Fold the central edges of the near layers out to the sides. Swing the triangular bottom flap to the rear.

27. Squash-fold the layers in the middle while folding the points at the top of the model down and out to the sides.

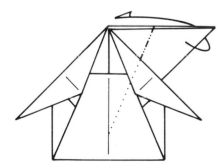 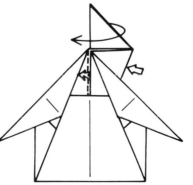 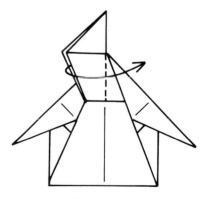

28. Mountain-fold the large flap at the top so that its lower edge lies along the vertical center line behind.

29. Reverse-fold the edge shown, keeping the two back layers together.

30. Fold the near flap on the left side over to the right side.

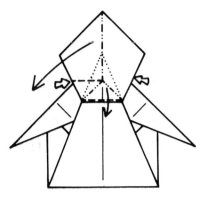

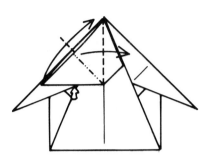

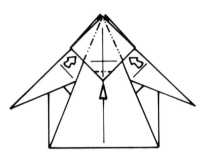

31. Pinch the top flap and swing it down to the left.

32. Squash-fold the flap upward.

33. Open-sink the bottom point of the square. Reverse-fold its side corners so that the upper edges lie along the center line.

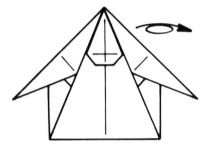

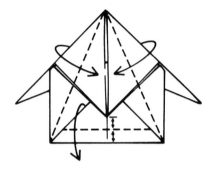

34. Turn the model over from side to side.

35. Fold the upper edges in to the center line. Fold down the bottom flap that is partially covered by the closed point, making the crease halfway between the closed point and the bottom edge.

36. Mountain-fold the tip of the bottom flap. Turn the model over from side to side.

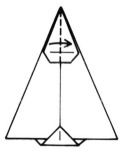

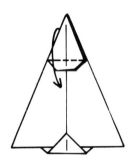

37. Fold the left flap over to the right side.

38. Fold one point down as far as it will go.

39. Fold one flap back to the left.

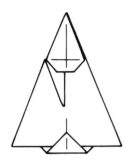 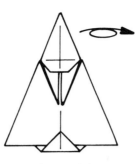 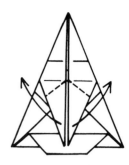

40. Repeat steps 37–39 on the right.

41. Turn the model over from side to side.

42. Fold the two flaps that lie along the center line up and outward with their top edges perpendicular to the outer edges.

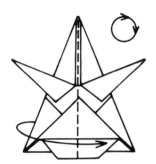

43. Fold the model in half lengthwise from left to right and rotate it a quarter turn clockwise.

44. Crimp the body about a third of the way from the left side. Pivot the head so that the nose (the rightmost point) moves down and the ears (along the back) move up.

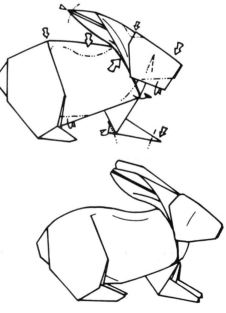

45. Enlarged view. Mountain-fold the edge of the ear; repeat behind. Reverse-fold the nose. Reverse-fold the hind leg; repeat behind.

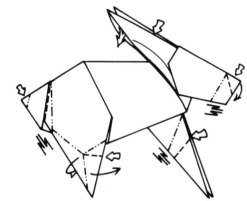

46. Press on the ears to flatten them and spread their layers slightly apart. Crimp the nose downward. Crimp the tail and reverse-fold the tip of it. Crimp the forelegs to angle them forward and fold a rabbit ear on each hind leg (it does not extend to the tip of each foot).

47. Round and shape the back and haunches. Blunt the tips of the ears with tiny sinks. Push in the top of the head to flatten it slightly. Narrow the head with a mountain fold at the jaw; repeat behind. Shape the face. Round the chest with soft mountain folds; repeat behind. Blunt the tip of each front foot with a reverse fold and fold the triangular corners at the elbows inside. Round the belly with a mountain fold; repeat behind.

48. The finished Rabbit.

RABBIT 119

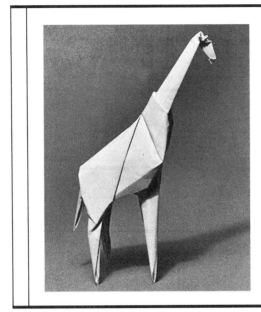

GIRAFFE

Use a square the same color on both sides. If only one side is colored, begin with the white side up for a colored model. Crease the vertical diagonal.

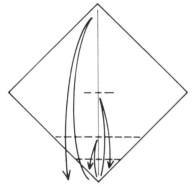

1. First bring the top corner down to the bottom corner, pinch at the center point, and unfold. Second, fold the bottom corner to the center point, crease, and unfold. Third, fold the bottom corner to the center of the crease just made, crease, and unfold.

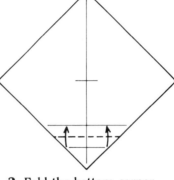

2. Fold the bottom corner up so that the lowest horizontal crease is aligned with the next crease above it.

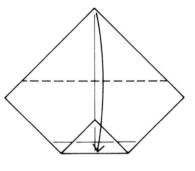

3. Fold the top corner down to the center of the bottom edge.

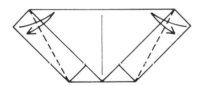

4. Fold in each side from the ends of the top and bottom folded edges, and unfold.

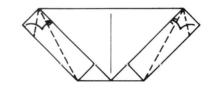

5. Fold each short upper edge to the creases just made. Then fold the sides in again along these creases, tucking them under the large front flap.

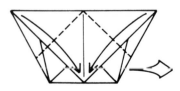

6. Fold the left and right upper corners to the center of the bottom edge.

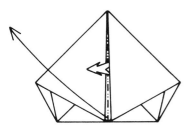

7. Enlarged view. Pull out and to the left the paper that lies behind the near flaps.

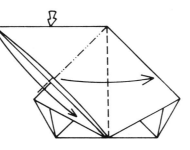

8. Squash-fold the large flap.

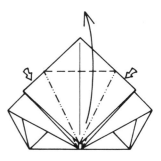

9. Petal-fold the flap.

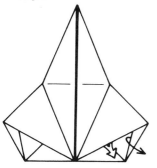

10. Pull the paper out from inside the lower right edges.

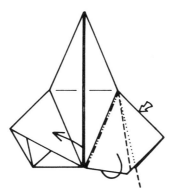

11. Swivel the paper on the right side to the left, pulling it under the layers near the center.

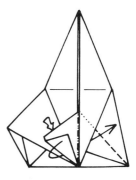

12. Swivel the paper left of the center back to the right.

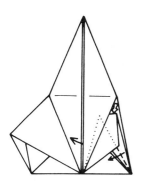

13. Swivel back to the left again along the existing crease.

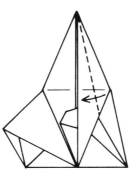

14. Fold the right upper edge to the center line.

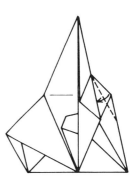

15. Fold the short right outer edge to the folded edge just made.

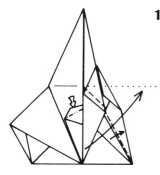

16. Fold the point of the near central flap upward to the right so that it is perpendicular to the vertical center line and is as far up as the layers will allow. The layers behind the flap will swivel and spread as this is done.

17. Swivel the edges shown.

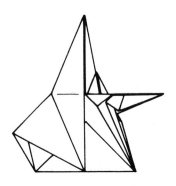

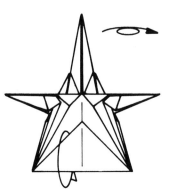

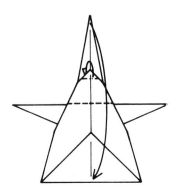

18. Repeat steps 10–17 on the left side.

19. Swing the triangular bottom flap to the rear and turn the model over from side to side.

20. Mountain-fold the upper part of the small closed tip into the model. Fold the top point down to the center of the bottom edge.

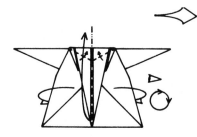

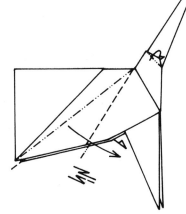

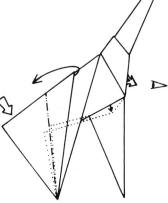

21. Fold the central flap up into a rabbit ear while simultaneously mountain-folding the left and right sides so that they come together. Rotate the model a quarter turn clockwise.

22. Enlarged view, from the side. Mountain-fold the small corner on the neck into the model. Repeat on the far side. Crimp the left end forward from the bottom corners to the base of the neck.

23. Reverse-fold the left corner along the interior layers indicated by the X-ray lines; then swing the raw edges to the left. Pull out the loose paper inside the chest and wrap it around the interior layers while unfolding the paper below it down over the top of the legs (see steps 24 and 25 for details).

24. This is a front view of the chest. Pull the two flaps downward as far as possible, allowing the small pleats to come out of their pockets . . .

25. . . . like this.

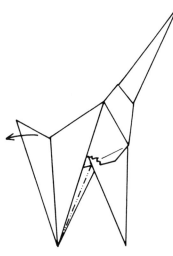

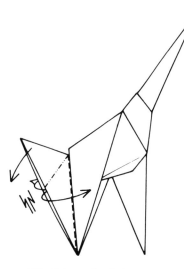

26. Swivel the left point farther left and down by rolling leftward the edges of the layers between the hind legs; the paper to the right of the mountain fold is drawn to the left as the point moves leftward.

27. Crimp the left point downward, folding the raw edges over the legs.

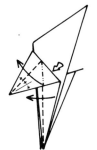

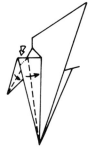

28. Swivel to the left, folding up two-thirds of the left point.

29. Swivel to the right, folding the left point in half.

30. Pull the left point upward allowing the paper to unfold.

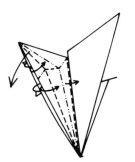

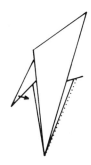

31. Pleat the paper as shown along existing creases to form the tail.

32. Tuck the pleated paper inside the legs.

33. Swivel the tail assembly to the right so that the pleats are hidden by the legs. The paper to the right of the legs is rolled out from the inside during this maneuver; the action is the opposite of step 26.

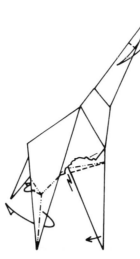

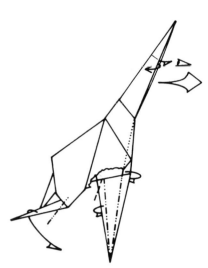

34. Reverse-fold the inner layers.

35. Fold a rabbit ear from each hind leg, turning it backward. Crimp each foreleg over the inner layer, adjusting slightly leftward the angle of leg. Fold and unfold the top of the neck.

36. Mountain-fold the hind leg down. Narrow the foreleg by mountain-folding each side. A small swivel forms a collar on the left side of the crimp on the inside. Repeat these steps on the far legs.

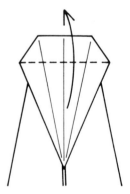

37. Inside view of the far front leg with step 36 completed.

38. A greatly enlarged view of the inside of the head area and a bit of the neck. Spread apart the folded edges that lie along the center line. Fold the top point down while opening the layers along the creases shown.

39. Fold the flap up at its widest point.

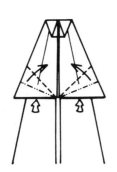

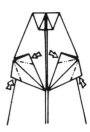

40. Fold the bottom edges to the center line and unfold. Pleat the tip.

41. Squash-fold the bottom corners.

42. Reverse-fold the corners of the squashed corners.

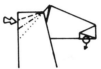

45. Spread open the ears as indicated by the push arrow and pull them down slightly. Pull the head down slightly . . .

43. Close the neck while reverse-folding the head downward.

44. Reverse-fold the left corner of the neck and then reverse it upward again (along the valley fold) so that the edges are even on top. Pull the lower jaw down slightly.

46. . . . like this.

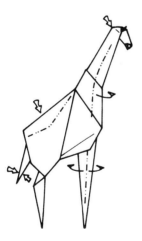

47. Round the neck by pressing the front in slightly. Press in the back of the head to round it. Squeeze the forelegs and tail slightly to narrow them. Press down the back from the base of the neck to the tail.

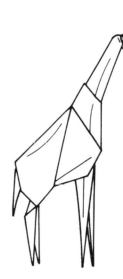

48. The finished Giraffe.

HORSEFLY

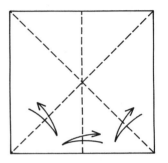

Use a large square of paper-backed foil. Begin with the white side up for a white fly with colored eyes. For greater realism, use green foil, color the white side black, and begin with the black side up.

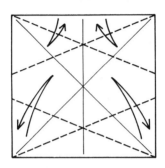

1. Crease the paper in half vertically and along both diagonals.

2. Crease the bisectors of the angles formed by the diagonals and the top and bottom edges.

3. Fold the lower left corner up to the right to touch the diagonal. Note that the crease of the fold intersects the left edge of the paper at the same place as an existing crease.

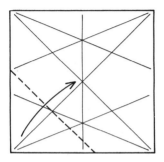

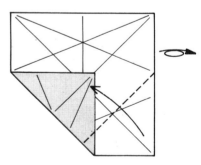

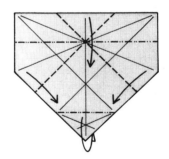

4. Fold the lower right corner up to match. Turn the paper over from side to side.

5. Mountain-fold the bottom point; note the reference points. Form a Waterbomb Base from the top of the paper, using existing creases as a guide.

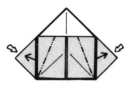

6. Reverse-fold the side corners inward, and the edges along the center line outward.

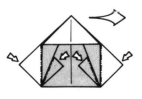

7. Reverse-fold the two corners on each side of the model.

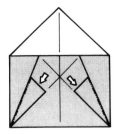 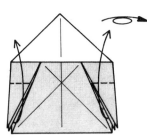 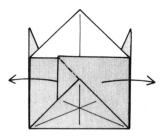

8. Enlarged view. Reverse-fold the remaining pair of corners.

9. Fold two flaps on each side upward. Turn the model over from side to side.

10. Pull out the corners of the square and pinch them in half.

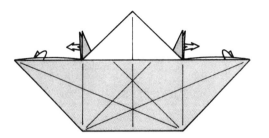 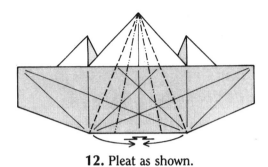

11. Pull to the outside the raw edges of the far side and release the trapped paper in the points as shown. Then flatten the paper into the position shown in step 12.

12. Pleat as shown.

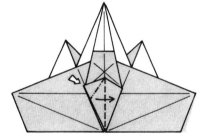

13. Pinch the lower portion of the pleat; note the location of the valley fold.

14. Squash-fold the flap.

15. Make a long, narrow petal fold.

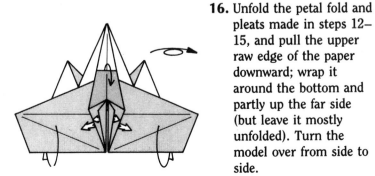 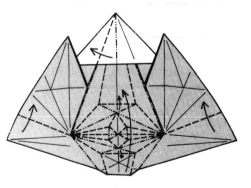

16. Unfold the petal fold and pleats made in steps 12–15, and pull the upper raw edge of the paper downward; wrap it around the bottom and partly up the far side (but leave it mostly unfolded). Turn the model over from side to side.

17. Refold on these creases.

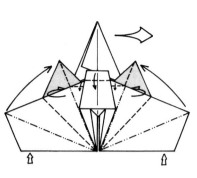

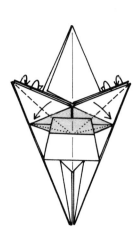

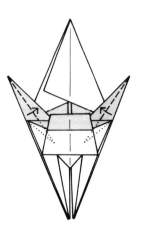

18. Pleat the sides as shown. Wrap the top of the central trapezoid downward.

19. Enlarged view. Reverse-fold three edges on each side as shown.

20. Fold one layer inward on each side.

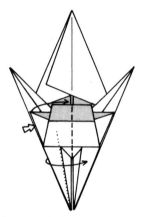

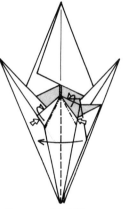

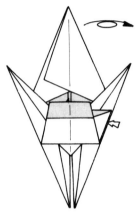

21. Squash-fold the indicated edge.

22. Reverse-fold the corners shown. Close the flap again.

23. Repeat steps 21 and 22 on the right. Turn the paper over from side to side.

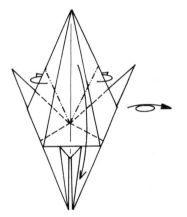

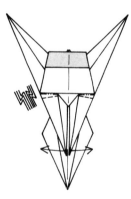

24. Bring downward the thick point at the top, forming creases as shown (see step 28 for the result). Turn the paper over again.

25. Crimp the two points (the wings) as shown.

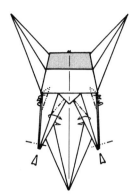

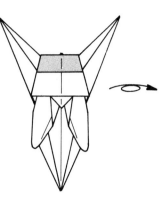

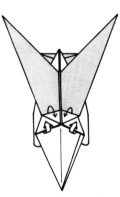

26. Open-sink the tip of each wing. Pull toward the center of the model the layers (front and back) that lie along the inner edge of each wing; flatten these layers into the configuration shown in step 27. Mountain-fold the outer edge of each wing from the place where it joins the body, tucking this edge inside; repeat behind on the far layer of each wing.

27. Turn the model over from side to side.

28. Pull out the trapped layers of paper.

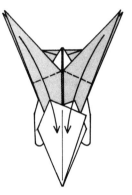

29. Fold one point down on each side.

30. Fold the next point down on each side, simultaneously pulling the outer near edges to the centers as shown by the long valley-fold lines.

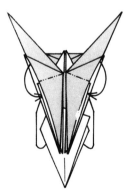

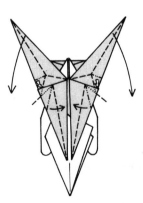

31. Reverse-fold the short points into the interior of the model.

32. Fold a rabbit ear from each remaining upward-pointing flap. Swivel inward the near outer layer of each downward-pointing flap.

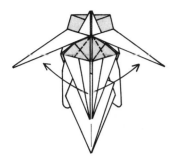

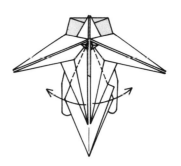

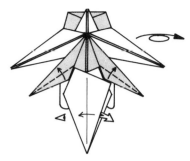

33. (The model is very thick now.) Fold the narrow points out to the sides.

34. Fold the remaining pair of points out to the sides.

35. Narrow that pair with valley folds. Open out the point at the bottom (the abdomen), making it three-dimensional, and turn the paper over from side to side.

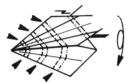

36. Detail of abdomen. At this point, the layers of the abdomen should form a three-sided pyramid. Crimp the pyramid all the way around, forming three concentric segments. Pleat the paper at the base of the pyramid to form the last segment. Turn the model over from top to bottom.

37. Fold up the bottom edges of the abdomen to round it; repeat behind. Pleat the wider front end to narrow it.

38. View of the wide end. Roll the pleat over twice to lock it (tweezers help here).

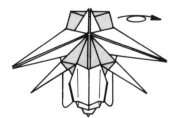

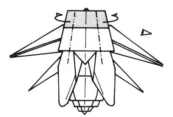

39. At this point, the abdomen is three-dimensional and the rest of the model is flat. Turn the paper over from side to side.

40. Gently shape the body with soft mountain folds as shown; don't make the creases sharp.

41. Side view of 40 rotated a quarter turn clockwise. Pinch the middle pair of legs and raise them up. Fold a double rabbit ear from each leg of the front pair. Crimp the head downward.

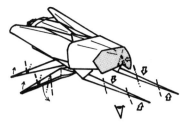

42. Crimp the middle and hind legs and feet. Form the forelegs and feet with reverse folds. Push in the region of the paper between the eyes and bring the short antennae through the opening from underneath.

43. View of the underside of the head, showing the antennae. Shape the body and wings for a proper pose.

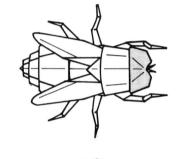

44. Three views of the finished Horsefly.

BLACK WIDOW

Use a large isosceles right triangle (made by cutting a square in half along the diagonal), black on one side and red on the other. Begin with the black side up for a black spider with a red "hourglass." Crease it in half and in fourths as shown.

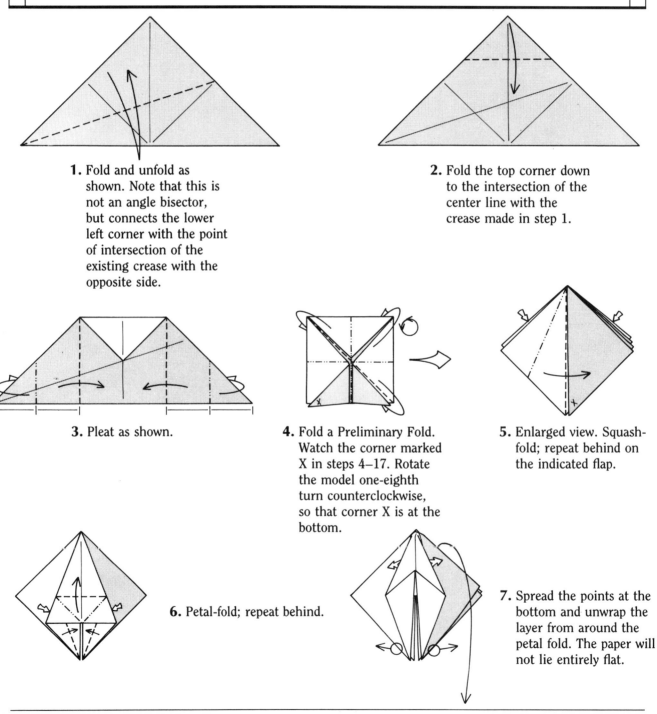

1. Fold and unfold as shown. Note that this is not an angle bisector, but connects the lower left corner with the point of intersection of the existing crease with the opposite side.

2. Fold the top corner down to the intersection of the center line with the crease made in step 1.

3. Pleat as shown.

4. Fold a Preliminary Fold. Watch the corner marked X in steps 4–17. Rotate the model one-eighth turn counterclockwise, so that corner X is at the bottom.

5. Enlarged view. Squash-fold; repeat behind on the indicated flap.

6. Petal-fold; repeat behind.

7. Spread the points at the bottom and unwrap the layer from around the petal fold. The paper will not lie entirely flat.

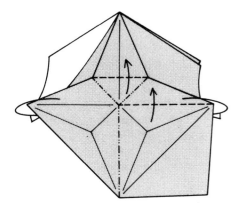

8. Refold, introducing the creases shown. Repeat steps 7 and 8 behind.

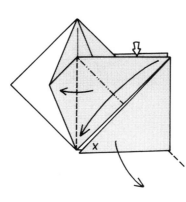

9. Squash-fold and pull flap X out; repeat behind.

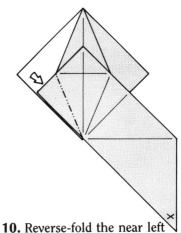

10. Reverse-fold the near left corner; repeat behind.

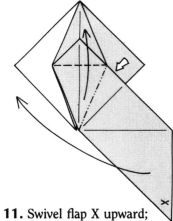

11. Swivel flap X upward; repeat behind.

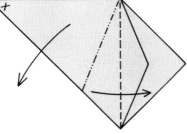

12. Pleat flap X; repeat behind.

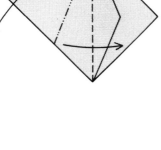

13. Reverse-fold the corner shown; repeat behind.

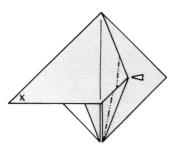

14. Open-sink the near corner shown; repeat behind.

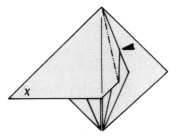

15. Closed-sink this corner; repeat behind.

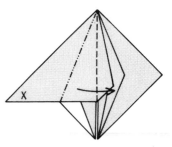

16. Pleat flap X again; repeat behind.

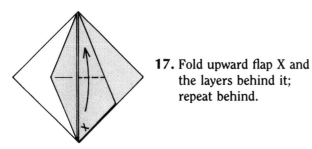

17. Fold upward flap X and the layers behind it; repeat behind.

18. Squash-fold to the left the corner shown; repeat behind.

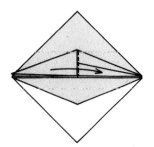

19. Fold one point downward; repeat behind.

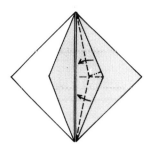

20. Fold a rabbit ear; repeat behind.

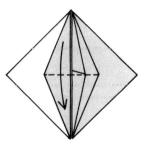

21. Fold one flap down; repeat behind.

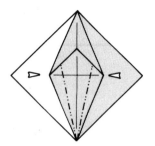

22. Open-sink the corners; repeat behind.

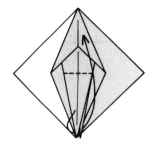

23. Lift up two points; repeat behind.

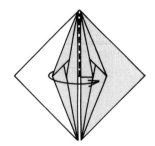

24. Fold all of the front layers over to the right; repeat behind in the other direction.

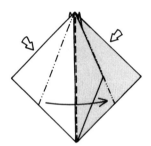

25. Squash-fold the left flap; repeat behind with the right flap.

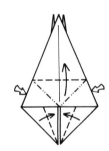

26. Petal-fold; repeat behind.

27. Unwrap the layers from around the petal fold as in steps 7–8 (only on the front, however).

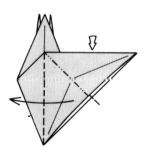

28. Squash-fold.

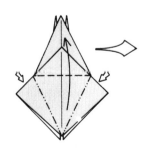

29. Petal-fold.

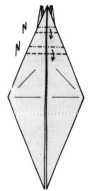

30. Enlarged view. Pleat the flap in two places.

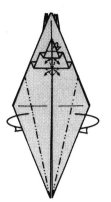

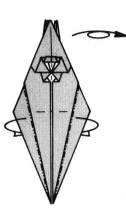

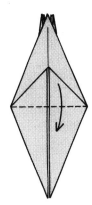

31. On each side, mountain-fold two layers together as one. Mountain-fold the tip of the pleated flap. Reverse-fold the edges that are under the pleats, opening them out to expose the color on the other side of the paper.

32. Mountain-fold one layer on each side. Turn the model over from side to side.

33. Fold down the short flap in the middle.

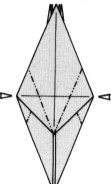

34. Open-sink the side corners.

35. Detail of the central section (the head). Pleat the flap upward.

36. Pull out two layers of paper.

37. Swing the flap over to the right and squash-fold the top of the left side.

38. Pull out two layers from the left.

39. Outside-reverse-fold the flap.

40. Squash-fold.

41. Fold the narrow flap down.

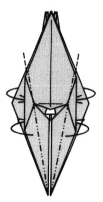

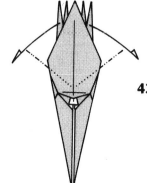

42. Mountain- and valley-fold the sides into the model.

43. Mountain-fold the indicated points out to the sides.

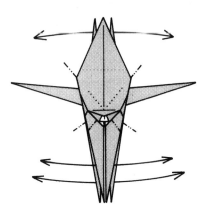

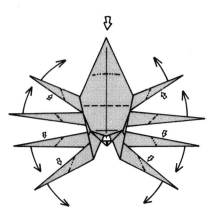

44. Reverse-fold the remaining six points out to the sides.

45. Reverse-fold all eight legs. Push in the tip of the abdomen and fluff out the sides by gently pulling apart opposite pairs of the edges that converge at the tip.

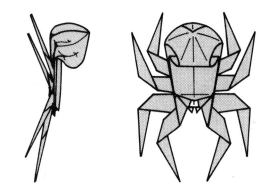

46. Two views of the finished Black Widow.

REINDEER

Use a large square of paper-backed foil. Begin with the white side up for a colored deer with white antlers.

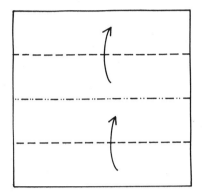

1. Pleat the paper into fourths horizontally.

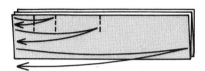

2. Crease the paper as shown. First, bring the left edge all the way over to the right edge, pinch, and unfold. Then bring the left edge to the crease just made, pinch, and unfold. Then bring the left edge to that crease, pinch and unfold.

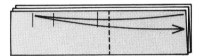

3. Now bring the right side over to the last crease made in step 2. Crease through all the layers of paper and unfold.

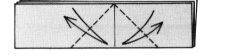

4. Crease through all layers.

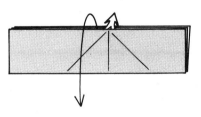

5. Open out the paper all the way, returning it to step 1.

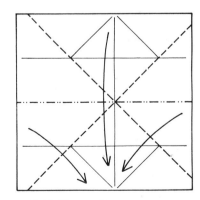

6. Fold an offset Waterbomb Base, using the existing creases as a guide.

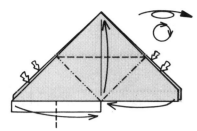

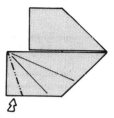

7. Push on the diagonal edges and bring the middle of the inner layer of paper up from the bottom to the top. The diagonal mountain folds already exist, and the valley fold will invert an existing mountain crease. Repeat behind. Rotate the model a quarter turn clockwise, and turn over the paper.

8. Crease angle quadrasectors through the two near layers. It will be easiest if you make the middle crease first and then use this as a guide for the other two creases.

9. Only the near half of the model is shown in steps 9–22, and all actions refer only to this half. Reverse-fold the bottom left corner on an existing crease.

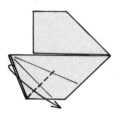

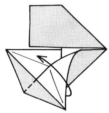

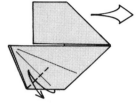

10. Fold down the left corner of the near flap as far as it will go (limited by the reverse-folded corner from the previous step).

11. Fold the corner back up to the left.

12. Fold the bottom edge upward on the crease made in step 10, but this time crease through both of the near layers. This crease will be used as a reference point in step 14.

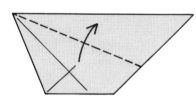

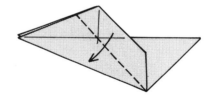

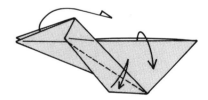

13. Enlarged view. Only the lower portion of the model is shown in steps 13–22. Fold the bottom upward on an existing crease.

14. Fold as shown. Note that the fold passes through the intersection of two existing creases (the vertical crease was made in step 10), and (look ahead to step 15 to see this) the top corner lies slightly above the horizontal crease.

15. Fold and unfold the triangle at the bottom of the model. Note that the crease does not go all the way to the upper left corner, but rather meets the edge of the paper where the edge crosses the horizontal crease on the layer behind. Pull out a single layer of paper from the right and swing the loose point at the left away and to the right.

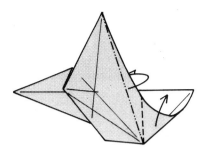

16. Form the mountain fold on an existing crease and flatten the model.

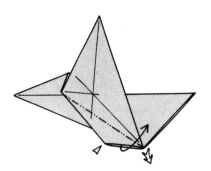

17. Open-sink the corner at the bottom of the model on the creases made in step 15. The two corners at the lower right are locked together, but as you make the open sink, they will come apart.

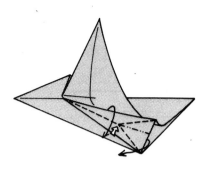

18. The sink in progress.

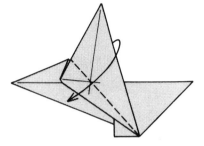

19. Fold the point back down to the left.

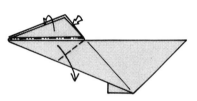

20. Pinch the near point at the left and swing it down.

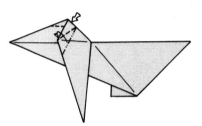

21. Narrow the top with a swivel fold so that the edges intersect on the horizontal center line (see step 22).

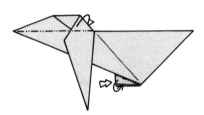

22. Mountain-fold the layers at the top into the interior of the model. Reverse-fold the small corner at the bottom right. Repeat steps 8–22 on the other side.

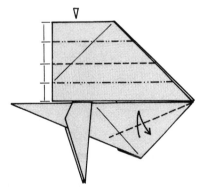

23. The entire model is now shown. Crease the bottom right through half of the layers; repeat behind. Divide the near half of the top of the model into fourths and open-sink it in and out.

24. Only the pleated part is shown. Note the position of the corner marked X in steps 24–35. Mountain-fold it up to the folded edge.

25. Top view of 24. The dotted line shows where corner X used to be. Push on the nearest folded edge and stretch the corner downward.

26. Corner X becomes visible again. Push in together the raw and folded edges and stretch the next double layer of paper down over corner X.

27. Pull out the edge from inside the pocket, and flatten the paper.

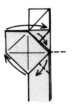

28. Fold upward the small square flap.

29. Unwrap around to the left the layers of the square flap; the paper must be partially unfolded to avoid wrinkling it. Flatten the model.

30. Pivot the pentagonal region as shown.

31. Fold a rabbit ear from the flap as shown.

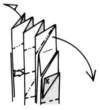

32. Corner X has reappeared. Repeat steps 25–31 on the other side.

33. Side view of 32. Push in the three top corners and stretch as far apart as possible.

34. Bring the points back together, incorporating the reverse fold shown.

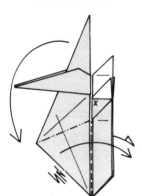

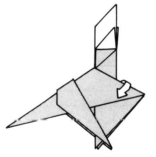

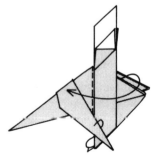

35. The entire model is shown again. Crimp the bottom left layers around the right half of the model (two in front, two behind); the top left structure will swing down.

36. Wrap one layer around to the front; repeat behind.

37. Open the right half of the model to the left. Only this opened portion is shown in steps 38 and 39.

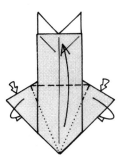

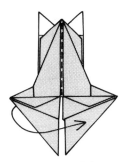

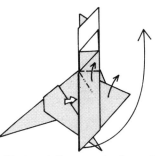

38. Petal-fold, using the existing creases as a guide.

39. Close the model again.

40. Partially squash the point up to the right; the point will not lie flat.

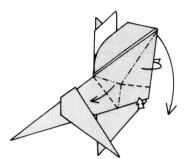

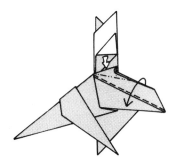

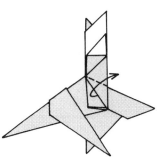

41. Bring it back down and pinch the indicated rabbit ear into position. The long mountain fold falls on an existing crease.

42. Squash-fold the indicated layer down and flatten the model.

43. Fold the flap upward again.

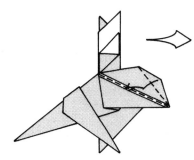

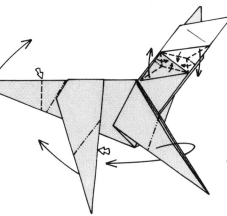

44. Fold the corner over and tuck the entire flap inside the pocket shown. Repeat steps 40–44 on the other side.

45. Enlarged view. Reverse-fold the tail in and out. Reverse-fold the hind legs, at the left. Mountain-fold the foreleg (at the right); repeat behind on the other leg. Form rabbit ears on the two triangular flaps at the top of the model; repeat behind.

46. Mountain-fold to the inside of the model the edges at the base of the tail. Reverse-fold the hind legs downward. Fold the foreleg downward. Fold a rabbit ear from each of the two remaining flaps at the top of the model. Repeat behind. Reverse-fold the head (and the extra layers wrapped around it) downward as indicated by the dotted line.

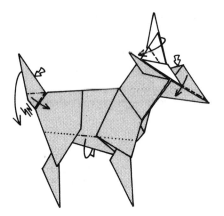  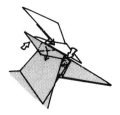

47. Crimp the tail down. Mountain-fold the chest and belly to the inside of the model. Fold the top antler downward. Reverse-fold the top corner of the nose and fold the rest of the flap downward. Repeat behind.

48. Carefully mountain-fold the thick edges at the rear of the neck to the inside of the neck. You will need to make a small swivel fold where the edge meets the antlers, forming a small collar behind them (indicated by the X-ray line). Fold the edges at the front of the neck inside as shown. Repeat behind.

49. Squash-fold the ear. Squash-fold the eye. Repeat behind.

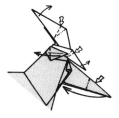

50. Fold the ear back to the left. Crimp the antlers upward. Reverse-fold the nose (there will be more layers on one side than the other). Repeat behind.

51. The finished Reindeer.

BUTTERFLY

Use a large square of paper-backed foil. Begin with the white side up. Crease it into thirds and halves horizontally, vertically, and diagonally.

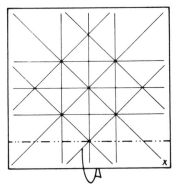

1. Mountain-fold the bottom one-sixth to the rear. Watch point X in steps 1–14 to maintain proper orientation of the paper as you fold.

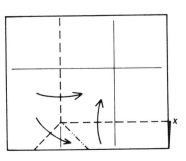

2. Fold a rabbit ear along existing creases.

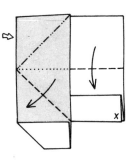

3. Squash-fold on existing creases.

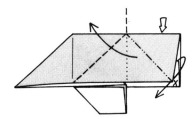

4. On the right portion of the model, swing the near layer of paper up to the left and pull point X slightly downward (the paper will not lie flat).

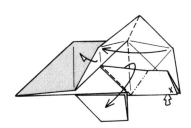

5. Swing the lower flap (which contains point X) down to the left using existing creases and squash-fold the right side of the model over to the left.

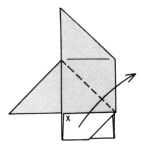

6. Fold the bottom flap over to the right.

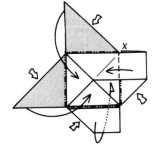

7. Reverse-fold all the "vanes" of the windmill shape in to the center of the model.

8. Turn the model over from top to bottom and rotate it an eighth turn clockwise so that the corner marked X is at the bottom.

9. Bring the side and bottom points of the near surface up to the top point, similar to a Preliminary Fold, but allow the points on the far side to flip out from the model.

10. . . . in progress.

11. Note the position of the long and short points and point X. Spread the layers as shown and flatten the model.

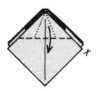 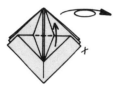 

12. Fold the near top point down and petal-fold the interior layers.

13. Fold the point up again. Turn the model over from side to side.

14. Fold the near top point down, petal-fold the interior layers, and fold it up again as in steps 12 and 13. Rotate the model a half turn.

15. Unwrap the layers from around the tiny Bird Base in the center. The model will not lie flat.

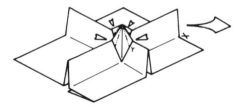 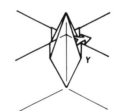 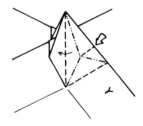

16. Open-sink the four corners shown.

17. Enlarged view of the central region. Pull out the paper on the flap shown (connected to the short side of the structure).

18. Refold as shown, symmetrically.

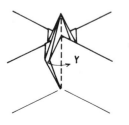 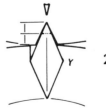

19. Fold one flap to the right; repeat on the other side of the ridge.

20. Open-sink half of the height of the central point.

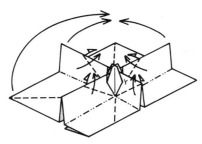
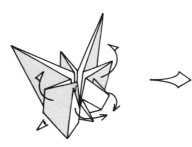
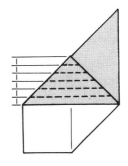

21. Gather the paper together by making an outside reverse fold on each of the four arms of the cross.

22. Bring the indicated layers together and flatten the model from side to side.

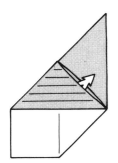
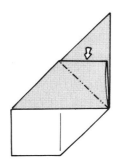
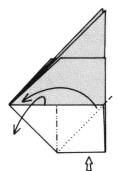

23. Enlarged view. Swivel the near layers as shown; repeat behind.

24. Reverse-fold the corner shown; repeat behind.

25. Crease the indicated triangle into sixths horizontally.

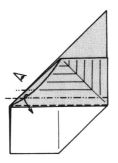

26. Undo step 24.

27. Spread and pleat the base of the creased trapezoid. A tiny bridge forms in the interior of the model . . .

28. . . . as shown here.

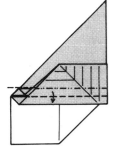
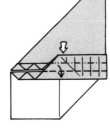

29. Repeat steps 27–29.

30. Squash-fold the remaining portion of the trapezoid, allowing the layers inside the left edges to spread flat.

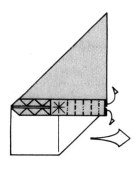

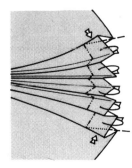

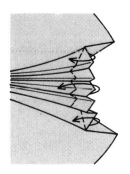

31. Spread out the edges of the pleated fanlike structure; then pleat the fan crosswise on existing creases and collapse it toward the center of the model as shown in steps 32–34.

32. Enlarged view. This shows how to collapse it. First, mountain-fold the edge to the rear on one continuous (existing) crease . . .

33. . . . then fold it toward you on the next existing crease . . .

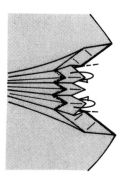

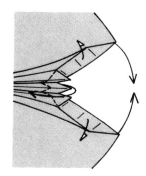

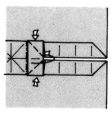

34. . . . then mountain-fold it to the rear again . . .

35. . . . then fold it toward you and bring the sides together; flatten it out.

36. Mountain-fold the remaining segment into the inside of the model, reverse-folding the top and bottom edges.

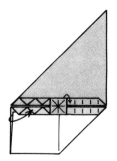

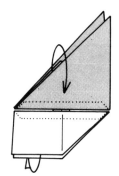

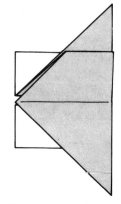

37. Perform a closed wrap on the top half of the pleated structure, bringing two layers from behind to the front. Tuck the bottom half of the pleated structure behind the loose white layer of paper. Repeat steps 25–37 behind.

38. Swing one flap down from the top in front and one flap up from the bottom in back.

39. Repeat steps 24–36 on the flap in the middle of the model.

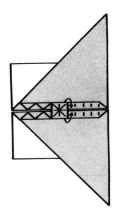

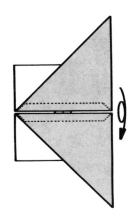

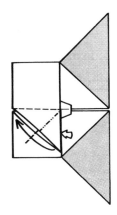

40. Perform a closed wrap on the top half of the pleated structure, bringing two layers from behind to the front. Repeat on the bottom.

41. Turn the model over from top to bottom.

42. Squash-fold the indicated flap.

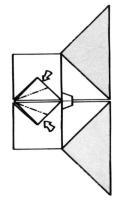

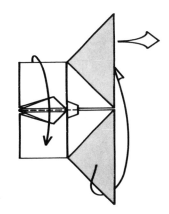

43. Reverse-fold the top and bottom corners.

44. Fold one flap down from the top in front and one flap up from the bottom in back.

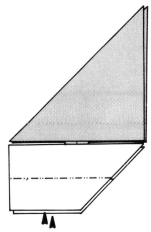

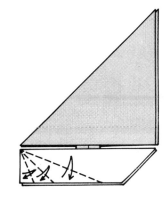

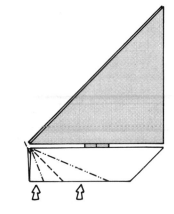

45. Enlarged view. Closed-sink the bottom half of each white flap upward.

46. Divide the angle of the upper left corner of the trapezoid into fourths with creases; repeat behind on all layers.

47. Reverse-fold each of the four flaps three times.

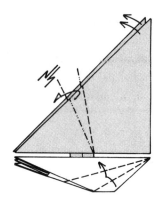

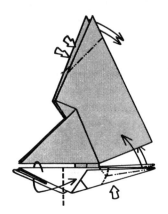

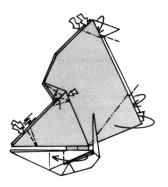

48. Pleat each wing. Narrow the antenna (bottom right) by folding over and over in thirds; repeat behind.

49. Reverse-fold the top of each wing. Fold the three points that lie in a cluster along the abdomen as far to the right as they will go; repeat behind. Fold a double rabbit ear from each antenna.

50. Crimp the trailing point on each wing (at the left) with two reverse folds. Reverse-fold the corner of the pleat that defines the leading and trailing wings; repeat behind. Reverse-fold the top of each wing asymmetrically. Shape the right edges of each leading wing with a mountain fold and a valley fold as shown; the edges of the paper go inside each of the wings.

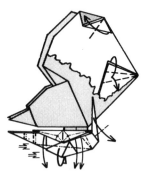

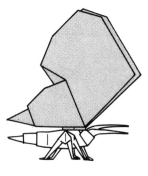

51. The near layer is shown cut away. Lock each wing together by tucking the point at the top into the pocket as shown. Lock the front of each wing by rolling the two inside layers of paper over twice. Pinch the three legs on each side and swing them down; crimp a foot on each. Crimp the abdomen to make segments. Narrow the abdomen with a mountain fold (this also locks the legs into place); repeat behind. Pleat one layer on each side to form an eye. Swing the antennae forward.

52. The finished Butterfly.

PRAYING MANTIS

Use a large rectangle of proportion 1:2.707, or approximately 7:19, the same color on both sides.

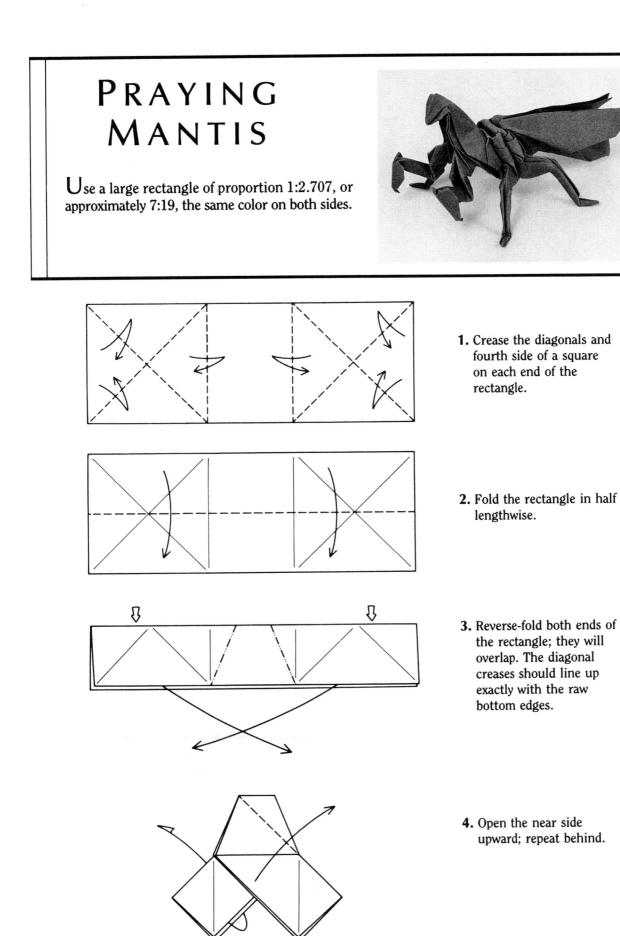

1. Crease the diagonals and fourth side of a square on each end of the rectangle.

2. Fold the rectangle in half lengthwise.

3. Reverse-fold both ends of the rectangle; they will overlap. The diagonal creases should line up exactly with the raw bottom edges.

4. Open the near side upward; repeat behind.

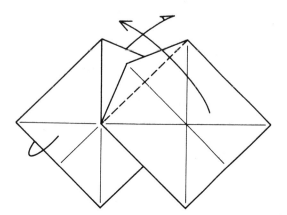

5. Fold the near and far squares upward along their creased sides.

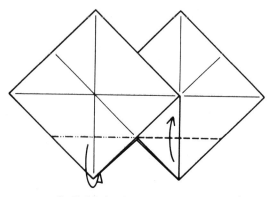

6. Fold the bottom right corner up halfway. Mountain-fold the bottom left corner up halfway.

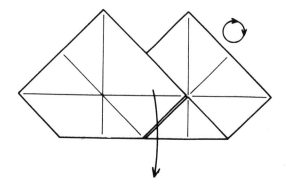

7. Swing down the near half of the model. Layers in the interior will prevent it from lying entirely flat. Rotate the model an eighth turn clockwise.

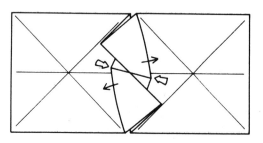

8. Press on the two three-way corners shown and flatten the model. The corners flatten and merge into a rectangle as the layers flatten.

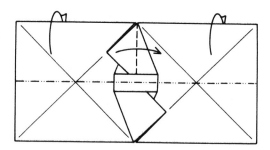

9. Swing the top flap to the right and mountain-fold the entire model in half lengthwise.

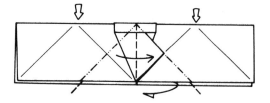

10. Squash-fold the left half of the model; repeat behind with the right half.

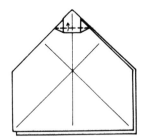

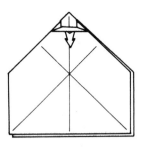

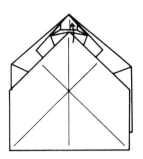

11. Fold the small flap upward as far as it will go; repeat behind.

12. Open the model and pull down the paper that forms the point inside the little hood. Reposition the point on the outside of the model.

13. Repeat behind and flatten the model.

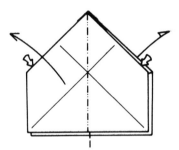

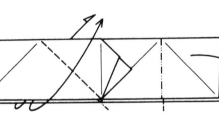

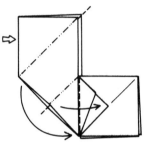

14. Pinch the near layer and swing it up to the left; repeat behind, to the right.

15. Outside-reverse-fold the left side. Inside-reverse-fold the right.

16. Reverse-fold the top corner on the left. Squash the lower portion of this flap. The top will rotate downward.

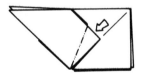

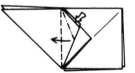

17. Reverse-fold the near corner as shown.

18. Squash the flap shown, allowing the inner layers to spread flat.

19. Swing two flaps to the right.

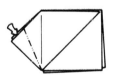

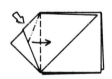

20. Reverse-fold the near corner.

21. Squash the flap, allowing the inner layers to spread flat.

22. Swing one of the large flaps back to the left.

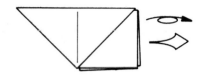 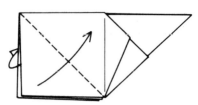 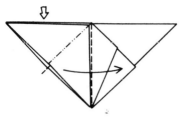

23. Turn the paper over from side to side.

24. Enlarged view. Fold the near flap along the diagonal; repeat behind.

25. Squash-fold the near left flap.

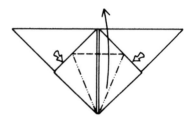 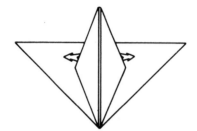 

26. Petal-fold the squashed flap. It has many layers, so this must be done carefully.

27. Pull out the trapped layers of paper.

28. There is more trapped paper inside the edges shown. Carefully pull it entirely out and lay it to the left to form a third Preliminary Fold type of flap.

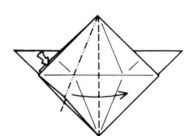 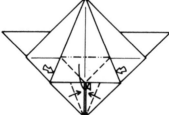 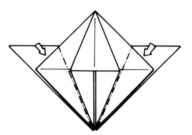

29. Squash-fold the middle flap.

30. Inside petal-fold the squashed flap.

31. Reverse-fold the corners as shown.

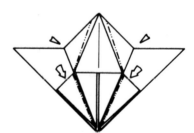 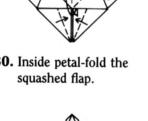 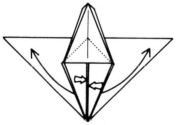 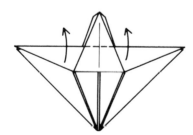

32. On each side, open-sink the upper corner, inverting it all the way to the center of the model. Note that the sinks do not extend all the way to the top point. Reverse-fold the lower corners.

33. Reverse-fold the two points shown as far as they will go to the left and right, respectively.

34. Lift up the near flap.

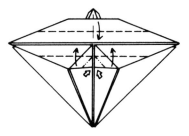

35. Fold the top edge down to the raw edge. Fold the lower edges up to the raw edges while squash-folding the inner corners.

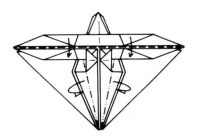

36. Fold down the top half of the horizontal flap. Mountain-fold inward to the center line the edges of the near flaps.

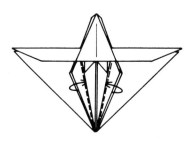

37. Fold in the next set of edges.

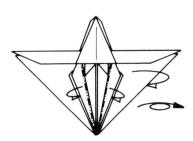

38. Mountain-fold the next set of edges. Swing the large flap from the right behind to the left, and turn the model over from side to side.

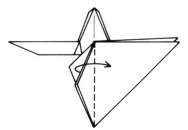

39. Swing two flaps over.

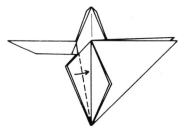

40. Fold the edges of one flap in to the center line.

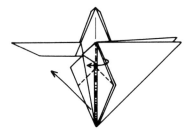

41. Swing one flap back to the left and incorporate the reverse fold shown.

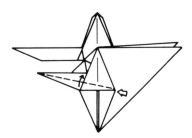

42. Fold the lower edge of the reversed flap so that it lies along the upper edge. At the right corner it will be necessary to spread and flatten the layers into a tiny gusset.

43. Simultaneously mountain-fold in three places.

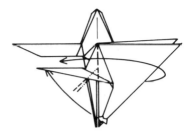 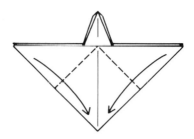 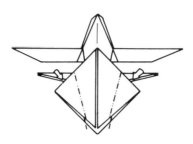

44. Reverse-fold the lower left point upward to match the other point. Swing the large flaps to the left and repeat steps 39–44 on the right side. Then fold one large flap to the right.

45. Fold the upper edge of each large flap to the center line.

46. Reverse-fold the corners. Note that the reverse folds do not go all the way to the bottom point.

 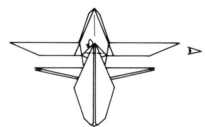 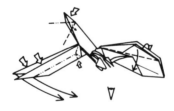

47. Mountain-fold the top edges to the center line. Reverse-fold the tips.

48. Mountain-fold the small corners into the pockets behind them; see step 49.

49. Side view. Fold the points individually.

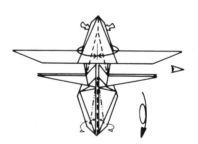

50. Opposite view of 48. Pinch the top of the model and bring the long flaps (the forelegs) together; the triangular area between the forelegs (the thorax) is kept flat by pressing it from the far side. At the bottom (the abdomen), fold the far layers away and raise the near layers toward you, bringing them together and pressing the abdomen tightly from both sides. Turn the model over from top to bottom.

51. Side view, rotated. Squash-fold the head down. Fold a double rabbit ear from the forelegs (at the left). Wrap the wings (at the right) around the abdomen.

52. Reverse-fold the foreleg.

53. Finish shaping the foreleg with a crimp, pushing in the corner at the top as it is formed. Make a small reverse fold on the tip. Repeat steps 52 and 53 on the other foreleg . . .

54. . . . like this.

55. Fold a double rabbit ear from the legs and reverse-fold the feet . . .

56. . . . like this.

57. View from 51. Spread the legs and push the tip of the abdomen in slightly to shape it. Turn the model over from top to bottom.

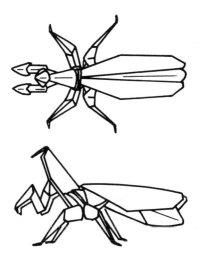

58. Two views of the finished Praying Mantis.

CRAB

Use a large square of thin paper-backed foil. Begin with the white side up for a predominantly colored model. Crease it in half vertically, horizontally, and diagonally.

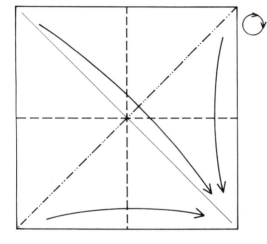

1. Make a Preliminary Fold. Rotate ⅛ turn clockwise, so that the four corners of the square are at the bottom.

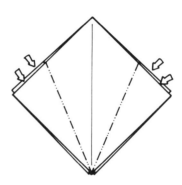

2. Reverse-fold the four corners to make a Bird Base.

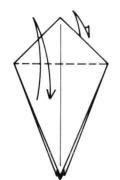

3. Lift the near flap up, crease, and return; repeat behind.

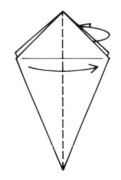

4. Fold one flap from left to right in front, and one from right to left in back.

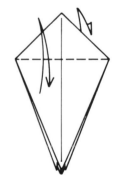

5. Repeat step 3.

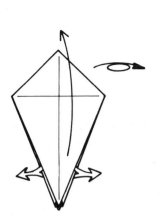

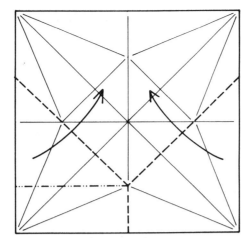

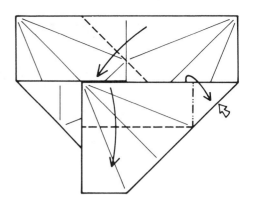

6. Unfold completely and turn the paper over from side to side.

7. Fold a rabbit ear along the existing creases, extending them as shown.

8. Swivel, using the existing creases.

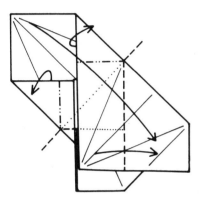

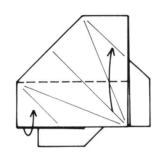

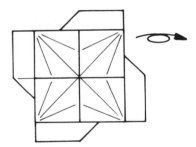

9. Spread the edges shown and bring the upper left corner down to the lower right.

10. Lift up two layers at the lower left, and flatten the model. The result should be a symmetrical windmill shape.

11. Turn the paper over from side to side.

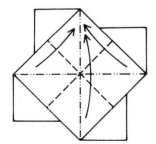

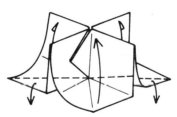

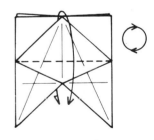

12. Form a Preliminary Fold from the square in the middle of the windmill. The model becomes three-dimensional.

13. Pinch the two corners at the sides and pull them downward; at the same time, squash the corners in front and back upward to join the points of the Preliminary Fold. Then flatten the whole model.

14. Fold one layer down in front; repeat behind. Rotate the model a half turn.

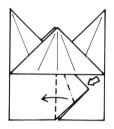 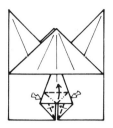 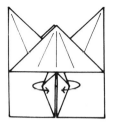

15. Squash-fold; repeat behind.

16. Petal-fold; repeat behind.

17. Perform a closed wrap on each side of the petal fold, bringing two layers from behind to the front. Repeat behind.

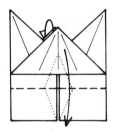 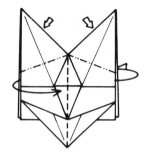 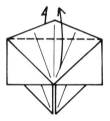

18. Fold the triangular center flap and the layers behind it as far down as possible; repeat behind.

19. Spread the raw edges on the left symmetrically and squash the top corner down. Repeat on the right, behind.

20. Fold the corner up; repeat behind.

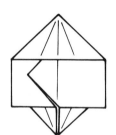 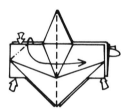 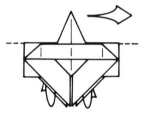

21. Repeat steps 14–18.

22. Bring one folded edge over to the right and squash the bottom edge upward while turning down the raw edge as it is stretched; repeat behind.

23. There are four bottom points; swing the two far points upward as far as they will go.

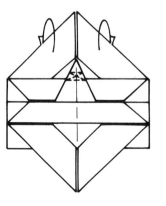

24. Enlarged view. Crease the thick point as shown. The lowest crease lies slightly under the raw edge of the layer behind it; the two diagonal creases meet the edges of the thick point at right angles at their upper ends; the upper horizontal crease connects the tops of the two diagonal creases.

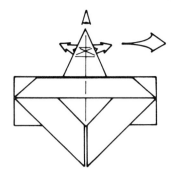

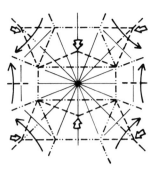

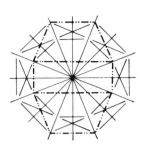

25. Open out the top of the thick point. (Try to keep the rest of the model from unfolding any more than necessary.)

26. Enlarged view of the top of the model. Here are the creases resulting from step 24. Make the creases shown into mountain folds (you will have to add the two long horizontal creases that define the central rectangle).

27. Refold the rest of the paper as in step 25. However, in the central region, push in just above and below the central rectangle (the other creases will tend to fall into place).

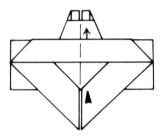

28. The rectangle is not pressed flat against the layers behind it here. Now bring the sides of the rectangle up and push down the middle, forming a kind of Waterbomb Base.

29. The top of the model looks like this. Press it flat.

30. Closed-sink the point shown, as far upward as possible. Do not repeat behind.

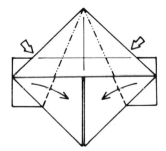

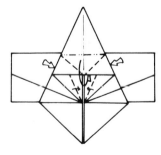

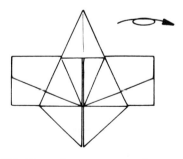

31. Reverse-fold the edges shown in to the center line.

32. Inside-petal-fold.

33. Turn the paper over from side to side.

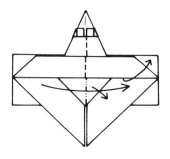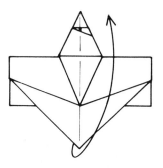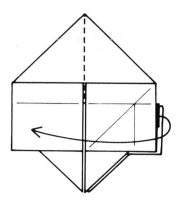

34. Bring one flap over from the left to the right; simultaneously, pull the raw edge of the paper (in the middle) out and to the right (this is the inverse of step 22).

35. Lift up one flap as high as possible.

36. Fold one full flap over to the left.

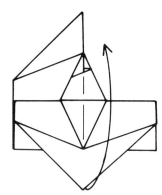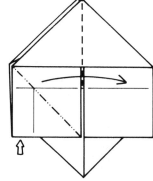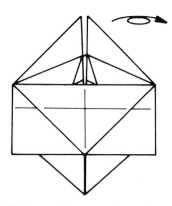

37. Lift up one flap as high as possible.

38. Squash-fold. Spread the interior layers symmetrically.

39. Turn the paper over from side to side.

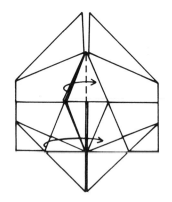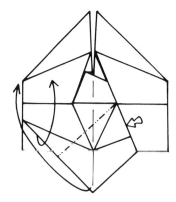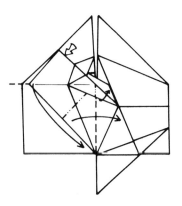

40. Fold three flaps over to the right.

41. Swivel the bottom corner up to the left.

42. Swivel it back down.

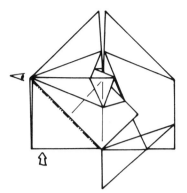

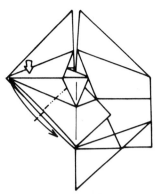

43. Reverse-fold the bottom left corner and tuck it into the pocket in the interior of the model . . .

44. . . . like this.

45. Reverse-fold the near left corner. The reverse fold runs all the way to the central axis of the model. This is only possible if the fold in step 43 was tucked inside the pocket.

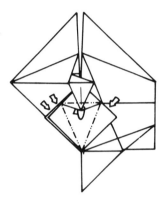

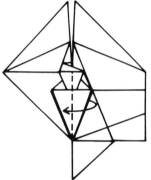

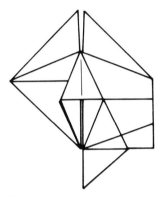

46. Mountain-fold the small triangle in the middle of the model and reverse-fold the three corners shown.

47. Fold three flaps back to the left.

48. Repeat steps 40–47 on the right.

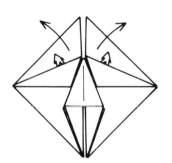

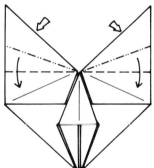

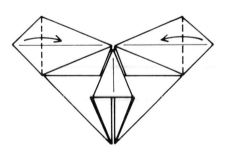

49. Pull the top corners up and out, releasing the trapped paper.

50. Squash-fold.

51. Fold the corners in.

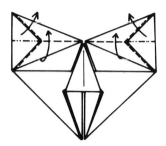

52. Fold a rabbit ear from the near layer of paper on each side.

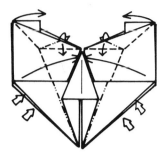

53. Reverse-fold the four edges at the sides and swivel the layers at the top.

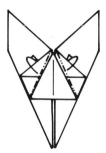

54. Mountain-fold the layers shown; repeat behind.

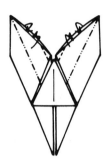

55. Mountain-fold the layers shown as far as possible into the interior; repeat behind.

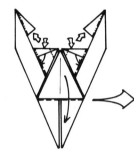

56. Reverse-fold the tips of the two long points (the claws). Tuck the thick points into the claws, reverse-folding their top edges. Fold downward the thick point in the middle.

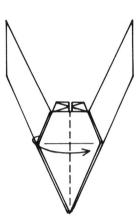

57. Enlarged view. Fold two flaps over to the right.

58. In steps 58–68 the claws are not shown. Bring one more flap over to the right and incorporate the reverse fold shown.

59. Narrow the point with a swivel on the near and far sides.

60. Mountain-fold the right side of the near flap.

  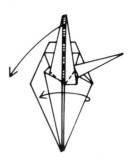

61. Lift up one point.

62. Fold a rabbit ear from the left flap, bringing two edges on the bottom and one edge on the top to the center.

63. Bring four lower right edges over to the left again and incorporate the reverse fold shown.

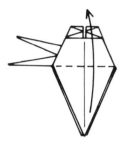 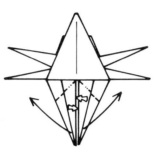 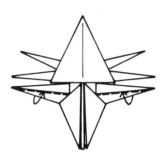

64. Repeat steps 57–63 on the right. Then lift up one point.

65. Reverse-fold the left and right near points out to the sides.

66. Fold the lower edges up inside.

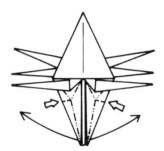 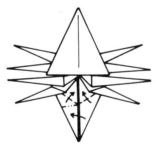 

67. Fold a double rabbit ear from the remaining pair of points. These eight points will be the legs.

68. Fold a rabbit ear from the bottom point.

69. In steps 69–72, the legs and upper body are not shown. Pull out two layers of paper on each side from the inside of the bottom rabbit ear and wrap them around the outside. Fold a rabbit ear on the top identical in size to the bottom one.

70. Squash-fold upward the flap of the lower rabbit ear.

71. Squash-fold the flap of the upper rabbit ear. Tuck the lower one behind the two folded edges on each side visible in step 70.

72. Swing the top rabbit ear down and tuck its edges into the same pockets that you tucked the bottom one into.

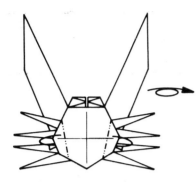

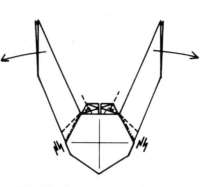

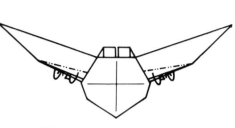

73. Mountain-fold the sides inward. Turn the model over from side to side.

74. The legs are not shown here. Crimp the claws outward. Reverse-fold outward the edges of the eyes (top middle).

75. Turn the near and far edges of each claw inside, swiveling at the crimp to form a small collar inside the shell.

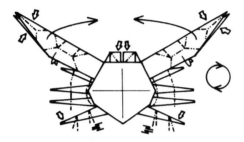

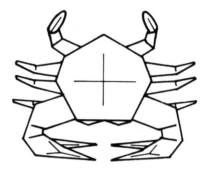

76. Pinch the tips of the claws so that the near and far points are symmetrical and become three-dimensional. Shape the claws with two rabbit ears along their length. Squash-fold the eyes. Bend the upper three pairs of legs to shape them. Crimp and squash the rear pair of legs. Rotate the model.

77. Two views of the finished Crab.

SOURCES

For information on origami organizations and publications and a list of domestic and foreign origami books and paper supplies that can be ordered by mail, send a self-addressed stamped envelope to:

The Friends of the Origami Center of America
15 West 77th Street
New York, NY 10024–5192

Or, call (212) 769-5635.